CONSUMER GUIDE®

Chevrolet
1955~1957

A '57 Chevrolet Bel Air Sport Coupe (*rear*) poses with the competition: Plymouth Fury (*foreground*) and Ford Fairlane 500.

Contents

Chevy closed the gap with Ford's legendary Model T by offering bigger, faster, brighter, and altogether superior cars for just a little more money. Then Chevy became a "Six at the Price of a Four." By the late Thirties, Chevy was Number 1.

With its powerful new V-8 and sensational styling, Chevy converted its image from dull and dependable to "The Hot One!" Not only was it the most-changed Chevy since the war, but also the most exciting car ever to wear the bow-tie badge.

This edition published by Beekman House, distributed by Crown Publishers, Inc., 225 Park Avenue South, New York, New York 10003.

Printed in Yugoslavia by Slovenija
h g f e d c b a

ISBN 0-517-65128-9

The ads said, "The Hot One's Even Hotter!" And it was, with up to 225 horsepower and new styling that featured a bold, full-width grille. Not surprisingly, Chevy had no trouble maintaining its customary position as America's favorite automobile.

The superbly restyled '57 debuted the now-famous 283-cubic-inch small-block V-8. Chevy ads boasted that it developed "1 h.p. per cu. in." with Ramjet fuel injection. The '57 is coveted not only as the last of the "classic" Chevys—but also as the best.

Credits

Photographers: Terry Boyce, David Gooley and Associates, Sam Griffith, Linda Hall, Bert E. Johnson, Vince Manocchi, Doug Mitchell. **Dealer books:** Bob Hofgren. **Special thanks to:** Bill Bodnarchuk; Chevrolet Motor Division; Charles M. Jordan, Head, General Motors Design Staff; Floyd Joliet, Adminstrative Operations, General Motors Design Staff; Ralph J. Kramer, Public Relations Director, Chevrolet Motor Division; Ron Pittman.

Before 1955:
The Making of
"USA-1"

America has been in love with the 1955–57 Chevy for some 30 years now. Why? Nostalgia mainly, plus sheer numbers: nearly five million built. As one writer put it: "Just about everybody had one once."

But there's more than that. Like other "great cars," Chevrolet's 1955–57 passenger models don't just mirror their time but transcend it, retaining an undeniable magic for those who knew them when, yet beckoning to enthusiasts not yet born when the last one rolled off the line.

An earlier generation of enthusiasts was quick to acclaim these cars "classic," a term once reserved only for certain prewar rarities. But it's appropriate for the Chevys, because though far more numerous, they're just as significant and memorable. They forever erased the "old fogey" image of General Motors' volume make, introduced a landmark V-8 that set a new standard of performance value, and left us with some of the sweetest, cleanest styling in postwar history. No wonder Chevy built so many.

Such intrinsic goodness partly explains their broad, devoted following, rare among mass-production models of any era. Only those history-making prewar Fords—Model T, Model A, and 1932 V-8—have inspired such enduring, widespread admiration. But while their fans are dwindling now, the Chevys seem to have more than ever. That's why you still see so many 1955–57s today, each a "solid gold" treasure to its lucky owner.

Yet it's important to remember that Chevrolet didn't set out to produce a "classic," but merely what one critic termed "an average automobile that offered good dollar value, was enjoy- able to drive, easy to maintain, and economical to operate. Certainly the high-performance editions were intended to strike a responsive chord in the hearts of horsepower aficionados, but the bread-and-butter models were built with Mr. Joe Average in mind."

Of course, Chevrolet had prospered with nothing *but* bread-and-butter cars since the early Twenties. By World War II it was GM's largest-volume division, had helped its parent achieve near total market dominance, and was more or less established as "USA- 1," the nation's most popular make. Depending on whether you use calendar or model year production, it first took that title from archrival Ford in 1927 or 1936. Regardless, Chevy's success rested on cars and trucks that one author characterized as "reasonably priced, reliable, easy to repair, easy to resell," offering "the masses a solid formula of value, comfort, and dependability backed by the strongest, largest, and wealthiest dealer network in the world."

Chevrolet's fortunes had been tied to GM's ever since 1918, when wheeler-dealer William C. Durant brought together the two concerns he founded (GM in 1908, Chevrolet in 1912). But their mutual, rapid growth in the Twenties and Thirties stems largely from president and board chairman Alfred P. Sloan, the revolutionary business practices he brought to GM—and thus to Chevy—and the astute designers, engineers, and managers he attracted. Among the last was William S. Knudsen, who became Chevrolet general manager in 1922 and began transforming a cheap car of dubious reliability into a rugged yet still affordable car of genuine quality.

Knudsen also went after Ford sales "one for one" through a vastly expanded dealer body and countless production improvements. Gradually, notes one historian, "Chevy closed the gap [with Ford's] legendary Model T by offering bigger, faster, brighter, and altogether superior cars for just a little more money."

And it didn't stop there. In 1929, two years after Ford began tooling the Tin Lizzie's long-overdue successor, Chevy became a "Six at the Price of Four" by switching to the overhead-valve engine, since lovingly enshrined as the "Stovebolt" because of its large, quarter-inch slotted head bolts. From 194 cubic inches and 50 horsepower, it grew to 216.5 cid and 85 bhp by 1937, when it was strengthened and completely redesigned. After adding five bhp for '41, it continued unchanged through 1950 as Chevy's sole powerplant. Aside from stout-hearted simplicity that would carry it all the way through 1962, the Stovebolt is important for prompting Henry Ford to introduce the industry's first low-price V-8. But even that couldn't halt the momentum, and by the time Knudsen replaced Sloan as GM president in 1937, Chevy was number one.

Several other features contributed to Chevrolet's prewar success: "Knee Action" independent front suspension (initially troublesome, like the Stovebolt, but just as quickly improved), clashless Synchro-Mesh transmission, all-steel "Turret-Top" body construction, hydraulic brakes. Chevy also benefited from GM's early emphasis on design, which emerged in the Thirties as a new and often decisive sales factor. Credit Harley J. Earl, who established GM's famous Art &

By World War II, Chevrolet was well entrenched as America's favorite auto: "USA-1." Dull, but always dependable, it appealed to millions on the strength of its practicality.

Colour Section, the first in-house styling department at a major auto-maker. He would be its head for three decades. His influence at Chevy was evident as early as 1930. "We can't afford big mistakes," he said later, "and we don't even like little ones." Thus, Chevy styling wasn't always adventuresome, but it was always saleable, unlike that of some rivals. And occasionally, it was brilliant: the Cadillac-inspired 1932 Eagle series and the smooth, Buick-like '41s were good-looking cars by any standard, the peak of prewar Chevy design.

Chevrolet continued its winning ways in the decade that both preceded and shaped its mid-Fifties "classics." Like other makes, its 1946 models were little more than warmed-over '42s (which had evolved from the popular '41s), but the huge postwar seller's market took every one. Additional minor facelifts followed for 1947–48, by which time volume was up to nearly 776,000 units.

Concurrently, the division weathered two unexpected leadership changes. First, general manager Marvin E. Coyle was replaced in June 1946 by Nicholas E. Dreystadt, his counterpart at Cadillac. But Dreystadt was felled by cancer in August 1948, and his successor, W. E. Armstrong, resigned because of illness after only a year. That brought Thomas H. Keating to the helm in 1949, the historic year when the industry completed its postwar design overhaul.

In line with GM's restyle, begun the previous season at Cadillac and Oldsmobile, the '49 Chevrolets were smoother, lower, and longer-looking, though their 115-inch wheelbase was actually an inch shorter than 1941–48.

Chevrolet's first postwar redesign emerged for 1949 *(top)*. An all-new body rode a one-inch-shorter wheelbase, but kept the same "Stovebolt" six, which had been rated at 90 bhp since 1941. A very mild facelift followed for 1950 *(above)*, but horsepower was 92, or 105 with Powerglide.

Featured were flush front fenders, closer-fitting rear fenders, broader grilles, curved windshields, and more integrated body lines. Models expanded with racy new Fleetline two- and four-door fastback sedans in Special and costlier DeLuxe trim. The Styleline Special series listed two-door Town Sedan, four-door Sport Sedan, Sport Coupe, and business coupe, all notchbacks. Styleline DeLuxe deleted the last but added the customary convertible and two four-door wagons—one with structural wood, Chevy's last woody, and a lookalike all-steel job, the make's first.

Yet for all their new finery, the '49s were still the same mundane people-movers Chevys had always been: as dull as the engine that powered them.

Though it was now called "Blue Flame," the old six was still spinning out 90 bhp at 3300 rpm, while the chassis hadn't changed much since the "Knee-Action" days. Ford, meantime, wrapped its equally aged flathead V-8 in contemporary slab-sided styling and adopted a completely modern suspension, thus polishing its long-time image as the "performance" car of the low-price field.

So while buyers liked the '49 Chevys, more of them liked that year's Ford, which admittedly benefited from an early sendoff (in June 1948). But though Dearborn won the model year production race by more than 107,000 units, Chevy took calendar year honors by almost 269,000 cars with a record total of nearly 1.1 mil-

lion, better than 40 percent up on 1948, remarkable in view of the stronger competition.

Chevy extended its lead for 1950 with two trend-setting "firsts" for the low-price field that would prove immensely popular: the Bel Air hardtop-convertible in the Styleline DeLuxe series, and optional two-speed Powerglide automatic. Accompanying the latter was a 235.5-cid six with 105 bhp, while the existing 216.5-cid engine somehow gained two extra horses. Styling stayed mostly the same, and Bendix "Jumbo-Drum" brakes arrived. With all this, Chevy built around 1.5 million cars for both the calendar and model years, besting Ford's market share 22.8 to 17.8 percent.

The following year saw industry-wide production cutbacks prompted by materials shortages due to the Korean conflict. Ford answered Chevy's 1950 exclusives, while "USA-1" made do with a mild, but pleasing facelift. Though both rivals lost market share, Chevy maintained a margin of 20.9 to 16.9 percent.

The '52 spread was 17.9 percent for Ford, 20.2 for Chevy. The reason? Ford was completely redesigned that year, the second time since the war, while Chevy had only another modest facelift. Had GM dropped the ball? Apparently so. In an age when buyers expected "all-new" looks and more horsepower almost annually, Chevrolet was still offering stylish but staid cars that didn't change much year to year. Lamented one Chevy exec: "Every time a prospective buyer saw one, he thought of his grandmother."

But GM had already recognized the problem. In December 1951, its Engineering Policy Committee had decided it had better "turn Chevrolet around" before it was too late. Given the industry's then-customary three-year lead times, this decision wouldn't reach full fruition until 1955. However, several interim developments suggested that "USA-1" was about to undergo a second transformation.

Chevy's Bel Air hardtop debuted for 1950, sending the competition scrambling to match it. Shown here in its 1951 guise (*top*), Chevy built over 100,000 hardtops for the model year. Chevrolet changed little (*bottom*) for 1952, the main distinctions being a toothier grille and the addition of extra chrome trim on the rear fenders.

They appeared for 1953 as the most changed Chevys in five years. Stylist Carl Renner dressed up the old '49 bodies with fresh sheetmetal below the belt, and divided windshields gave way to one-piece glass on most models. Fastback sedans were canceled due to declining sales, and the lineup was reordered into low-price One-Fifty, mid-range Two-Ten, and top-line Bel Air series. The smaller six was scrapped, and higher compression boosted the 235 to 105 bhp with stickshift (7.1:1) or 115 with Powerglide (7.7:1). The latter was also aided by new aluminum pistons (replacing cast iron) and insert-type rod bearings plus a more modern, pressurized lubrication system. Manual-transmission engines would get these changes for '54. All this reflected the presence of new chief engineer Edward N. Cole, who arrived in May 1952 from Cadillac, where he'd teamed with motor master Harry F. Barr on that division's milestone high-compression overhead-valve V-8 of 1949.

But the most visible symbol of Chevy's borning metamorphosis was the Corvette roadster, the 1953 Motorama "dream car" that went into very limited production late that year. Boasting a 150-bhp six with triple carburetors and 8:1 compression, the sleek, fiberglass-bodied two-seater left no one thinking of grandmother, and the excitement it spread over the regular Chevy line was like nothing the division had ever seen—just what the sales force wanted.

It was also what they needed. Determined to regain sales supremacy, Ford launched an all-out production "blitz" in 1953 as the industry shifted back into high gear with the end of the Korean War. Forced to sell cars they hadn't ordered, Ford dealers resorted to heavy discounting. Chevy had no choice but to follow suit, and the race was on. By 1954, the resulting buyer's market found Chrysler Corporation reeling and the independent producers moribund as Chevy and Ford publicly argued over sales figures. The market share gap was smaller than ever: 25.7 percent for Chevy, 25.3 percent for Ford.

Their '54 products were as closely matched. Though both wore only modest facelifts, Ford retired its old flathead V-8 in favor of the fine new overhead-valve "Y-block" engine, arriving with 239 cid and 150 horse-

power. It also adopted ball-joint front suspension. Chevy replied with more chrome and a fortified "Blue Flame" packing 115 bhp with stickshift (same as that year's 223 Ford six) or 125 with Powerglide. Model choices expanded as a four-door Bel Air Townsman wagon joined the carryover One-Fifty and Two-Ten Handyman models. Also returning from '53 were two- and four-door sedans in each series, One-Fifty utility sedan, Two-Ten Delray club coupe (a spiffy two-door sedan), and Bel Air convertible and Sport Coupe hardtop. New options included power brakes and power front seat and windows.

Despite its recent lack of product pizzazz and Ford's hard press,

The '53s (top) were heavily facelifted, and sported two-toning on the rear flanks of the Bel Air, which had blossomed into a four-model top-of-the-line series. Horsepower was upped to 105 with manual shift, 125 with Powerglide. Indicative of its success, the 30-millionth Chevy (bottom) was built on December 28, 1953—a '54 Bel Air convertible.

Chevrolet had somehow remained "USA-1." Now its all-new '55s were ready, and they couldn't have been better timed. Another history-making year was in the offing, and the first of the "classic" Chevys would set Detroit on its ear. A national love affair was about to begin.

1955:
"New Look!
New Life!
New Everything!"

The '55 Bel Air convertible — shown here with wheel covers, front fender shields, and sill moldings. (Owner: Archie L. Packard, Jr.)

The brochure blasted: "'Show Car' Styling at its Beautiful Best!" That was no exaggeration. The new look and the new V-8 made the 1955 model not only the most changed Chevy since the war, but also the most exciting car ever to wear the bow-tie badge.

T he 1955 Chevrolet was one of those happy cars whose whole exceeded the sum of its parts. Completely redesigned, with pretty styling and the option of a potent new V-8, it was not just the most changed Chevy since the war but the most exciting car ever to wear the bow-tie badge. "New Look! New Life! New Everything!" blared the brochures. "'Show Car' Styling at its Beautiful Best!"

That was no exaggeration, and the public loved it. Detroit produced over 7.1 million cars for model year '55, a record that would stand until 1963. Chevrolet built some 1.7 million of them—nearly 24 percent—to capture fully 44 percent of the low-price market.

Of course, most every make did well that season because most were "all-new" or nearly new, and Chevy's revitalized Ford and Plymouth rivals also tallied production gains of some 400,000 units over 1954. Yet more than 30 years later, it's the Chevy that's remembered most.

This timelessness derives from a basic design integrity unusual among mass-market Detroiters, which tend to

be compromises hashed out with one eye on the sales charts and the other on the bottom line. Not that a great many designers and engineers didn't have a hand in the '55 Chevy. But as one writer observed: "It definitely wasn't a car by committee. One man shepherded the ['55] through all its many stages, from first pencil line to running automobile. And that man was Edward Nicholas Cole."

Chevrolet had just started on its '55s when GM president Charles E. Wilson, future president Harlow H. Curtice, and Louis C. Goad interviewed Cole about becoming Chevy's manufacturing manager. He declined. "I didn't think the product was exciting enough," he said later. But management had just decided to "turn Chevrolet around," so they asked if he'd like to take over from Edward H. "Crankshaft" Kelley as division chief engineer. Cole said he would, if Kelley would step aside. Kelley obliged, becoming manufacturing chief, and Cole set up shop in May 1952.

Soon afterwards, GM chairman Alfred P. Sloan asked Cole about his plans for Chevy Engineering. Cole

wanted more staff—much more. Sloan agreed, and the department soon ballooned from 850 to 2900 employees. Later, Wilson laughingly told Cole, "I'll bet that's the first time you ever had your plans approved without submitting them."

Cole needed the help. Because an all-new Chevy was more or less as-

sumed by this point, a lot of work would have to be done quickly if he hoped to have it ready for '55. He also knew it would need a V-8 to provide the youthful performance that would transform Chevy's reputation for trustworthy but tepid cars.

As it turned out, Kelley was already working on one, basically a scaled-down, 230-cubic-inch version of the overhead-valve 1949 Cadillac V-8 that Cole had designed with Harry F. Barr. But Cole rejected it as too rich for Chevy's production budget, while an expected lack of power precluded a small V-6 created in 1947 by John Dolza of GM's Central Engineering Staff. There was now little time left for

Opposite page: Clare MacKichan *(top)*, Chevy design studio head, was partly responsible for the clean, uncluttered lines of the '55. Chevy preferred to call the Bel Air hardtop *(bottom)* a "Sport Coupe." *This page:* Some of the lines of the production '55 model can be seen in this styling study *(above)*, the "Grand Prix." This Bel Air convertible *(below)* is V-8 powered (note the "V" emblems below the taillights).

alternatives. With all the development phases involved, Cole would have just 15 weeks to devise his new engine.

So he promptly called his friend Barr, who came over from Cadillac to become assistant chief engineer a month after Cole joined Chevrolet. Together with Kelley, they not only beat the deadline but crafted an engine so good that it's still around today (albeit with numerous modifications made possible only by subsequent technological developments).

How'd they do it? As Cole reflected in 1974: "You just *know* you want five main bearings—there's no decision to make. We knew that a certain bore/stroke relationship was the most compact. We knew we'd like a displacement of 265 cubic inches, and that automatically established the bore and stroke [3.75 x 3.00 inches]. And we never changed any of this. We released our engine for tooling direct from the drawing boards—that's how crazy and confident we were."

Cole's "whole concept" for the '55 Chevy "was built around lighter components," and the new V-8 was no exception. Pushrods, for example, were hollow, and valve guides were integral with the cylinder heads, which were die-cast and completely interchangeable. The intake manifold provided a common water outlet to each. A short stroke meant short connecting rods (just 5.7 inches center distance) and pressed-in piston pins eliminated the need for a slitted rod and a locking bolt. Instead of working off a common shaft, each rocker arm was independent, assembled over a valve stem and pushrod retained by a fulcrum ball and lock nut, so deflection of one rocker wouldn't affect the others. With either mechanical or hydraulic lifters, the valves were lashed by simply turning the nut. A bonus was reduced reciprocating mass for higher maximum rpm.

Accordingly, Chevy specified three-ring, slipper-type "autothermic" aluminum pistons, with a circumferential expander for the single oil ring provid-

This 1955 Bel Air Sport coupe (*top*) is optioned with the gasoline filler guard, door handle shields, and license plate frames. The dual exhausts (*far left*) suggest this car has the 180-bhp "Power Pack," complete with Rochester four-barrel carb. The dash (*left*) sported two fan-shaped clusters for a "twin-cowl" Corvette look. (Owner: Bill Curran)

ing axial and radial force to control oil burning. Instead of alloy iron, the crankshaft was made of pressed forged steel, and newly developed forging techniques enabled it to be comparatively short for low torsional vibration with no sharp peaks; a harmonic balancer eliminated remaining vibration. Main bearings of equal diameter carried maximum load in their lower halves by omitting the customary oil groove, which reduced wear and doubled capacity. Exhaust manifolds were routed near the top of the heads, the passages flared up and out "ram's horn" style. Ports were fully water-jacketed for better heat dissipation around valve seats.

Chevy saved more weight with novel stamped-metal rocker arms and a splash lubrication system that eliminated separate and costly oil feeder

lines. The former, originated by Pontiac engineer Clayton B. Leach, was borrowed from that division's slightly larger new 1955 V-8, which was designed at about the same time and shared Chevy's valvetrain layout. This in turn suggested forcing oil up through the hollow pushrods to a hole in the rocker and out onto the top, thus lubricating the ball surface and valve stem. It also eliminated the need for oil passages in the head. Said Barr: "The ball was mounted onto a stud that was pressed into the cylinder head. These were all new ideas, and very good as far as automation was concerned."

Asked whether the Chevy V-8 pioneered any major breakthrough, Cole reflected, "If so, it was when we decided to make the precision cylinder blocks [with] an entirely different casting technique. We used the green-

sand core for the valley between the bores. . .to eliminate the dry-sand core so that we could turn the block upside down. We cast it upside down so the plate that holds the bore cores could be accurately located. This way, we could cast down to $5/32$ jacket walls." Originated by Dolza with his stillborn V-6, the technique made for an unheard-of degree of manufacturing precision.

Though only the second V-8 in Chevy history (the first was a short-lived late-Teens engine), the 265 was a landmark: 30 percent more powerful and 40 pounds lighter than the old six, a tribute to its careful engineering. Named "Turbo-Fire," it arrived with 8.0:1 compression and a rated 162 horsepower with two-barrel carburetor. A "Power Pack" version was added during the year as an option for all but wagons, with a smashing 180

This is what a well-dressed 1955 Chevrolet Bel Air convertible (*top*) looks like, featuring—among its many options—the ever-popular Continental tire carrier. This close-up (*above*) gives a good view of three popular extra-cost dress-up items: front fender shield, wheel cover, and the bumper-mounted fender guard. Chevrolet called its sensational new 265-cubic-inch V-8 (*right*) the "Turbo-Fire." And that it was, with 162 or 180 horsepower. (Owner: Bud Manning)

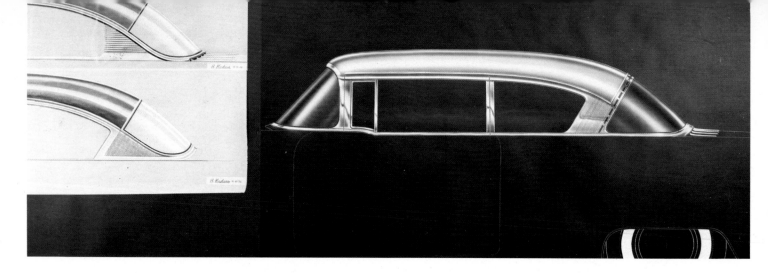

bhp via dual exhausts and Rochester four-barrel carb. Meantime, higher compression and minor internal changes brought the venerable "Blue Flame Six" to 123 bhp with stickshift and 136 with automatic, still with one-barrel carburetor.

Both six and V-8 could be teamed with one of three transmissions. The standard three-speed column-shift manual pulled a 3.70:1 rear axle, while the extra-cost Borg-Warner overdrive —the unit's first appearance on a GM car—had 4.11:1 gearing. Marketed as "Touch Down" overdrive, it dropped engine speed by 22 percent from 31

mph and up. Optional Powerglide automatic returned with a 3.55:1 axle.

Besides his V-8 work, Barr supervised development of a brand-new chassis and drivetrain, again with weight-saving always in mind. What emerged was conventional but modern and quite a departure for Chevrolet. Though wheelbase remained at 115 inches, the '55 frame was 18 percent lighter and 50 percent stiffer than previous Chevy chassis, according to Cole, with less unsprung weight and wider-spaced siderails for better stability. "We got away from the heavy torque-tube drive and went to [open]

Hotchkiss drive," he said. "We went to a Salibury-type [rear] axle instead of the banjo type...ball-joint front suspension [and] tubular frame." The last actually referred to box-girder siderails. Convertibles got a central X-member for the extra stiffness that body style requires.

Trumpeted as "Glide-Ride," the new front suspension was described as a "spherical-joint design" (to avoid Ford's "ball-joint" term) with "bearing surfaces of a new plastic material which is exceptionally long-wearing." Geometry comprised classic, unequal-length upper and lower A-arms acting

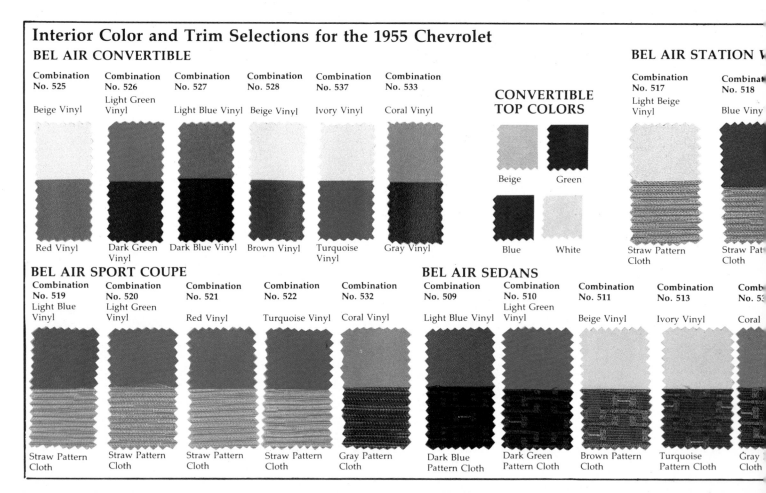

Interior Color and Trim Selections for the 1955 Chevrolet

BEL AIR CONVERTIBLE

Combination No. 525	Combination No. 526	Combination No. 527	Combination No. 528	Combination No. 537	Combination No. 533
Beige Vinyl	Light Green Vinyl	Light Blue Vinyl	Beige Vinyl	Ivory Vinyl	Coral Vinyl
Red Vinyl	Dark Green Vinyl	Dark Blue Vinyl	Brown Vinyl	Turquoise Vinyl	Gray Vinyl

CONVERTIBLE TOP COLORS

Beige Green

Blue White

BEL AIR STATION W...

Combination No. 517	Combinat... No. 518
Light Beige Vinyl	Blue Viny...
Straw Pattern Cloth	Straw Pat... Cloth

BEL AIR SPORT COUPE

Combination No. 519	Combination No. 520	Combination No. 521	Combination No. 522	Combination No. 532
Light Blue Vinyl	Light Green Vinyl	Red Vinyl	Turquoise Vinyl	Coral Vinyl
Straw Pattern Cloth	Straw Pattern Cloth	Straw Pattern Cloth	Straw Pattern Cloth	Gray Pattern Cloth

BEL AIR SEDANS

Combination No. 509	Combination No. 510	Combination No. 511	Combination No. 513	Comb... No. 5...
Light Blue Vinyl	Light Green Vinyl	Beige Vinyl	Ivory Vinyl	Coral
Dark Blue Pattern Cloth	Dark Green Pattern Cloth	Brown Pattern Cloth	Turquoise Pattern Cloth	Gray Cloth

on coil springs wound around life-sealed, double-acting hydraulic shock absorbers. Out back was the familiar live axle on parallel, longitudinal, semi-elliptic leaf springs, but the springs were nine inches longer (58 inches), wider (two inches), and newly mounted outboard of the main frame rails, thus dictating diagonal shock placement. Lube-free rear "spring leaf-end liners of impregnated webbing" were also featured. With the wider chassis and 6.70 x 15 four-ply tires (now tubeless as standard), track was 58 inches front, 58.8 inches rear.

Other mechanical highlights in-cluded switching from six- to 12-volt electrical system and adoption of recirculating-ball-and-nut steering with 20:1 ratio. The self-energizing, 11-inch-diameter "Jumbo Drum" brakes returned with new lube-free nylon bushings.

Because Chevy was GM's biggest seller, styling for the all-new '55 was carefully considered. Pierre Ollier, a former body designer in the compa-ny's commercial vehicle studios, re-called that serious design work got underway at about the same time as engineering, "around June 1952, at the GM Styling Building on Milwau-

Top row: Designers experimented with many different window treatments (*left*) for the 1955 Chevrolet. As shown here, the "Flight Sweep" wraparound windshield was already decided upon, but the rear window/C-post arrange-ment obviously wasn't. Splashy two-toning was all the rage by 1955, and Chevy wasn't about to be outdone by the competition, as demonstrated by these two Bel Airs, a two-door sedan (*center*) and a Sport Coupe (*right*). The former, with the top one color and body another, features the "Regular Two-Tone," while the latter sports the "Special Two-Tone," with the roof color splashed onto the rear part of the body as well. As was the practice then, chrome trim separated the colors.

NOMAD STATION WAGON

Combination No. 541

Beige Vinyl

Green Waffle Pattern Vinyl

Combination No. 544

Beige Vinyl

Red Waffle Pattern Vinyl

Combination No. 552

Ivory Vinyl

Gray Waffle Pattern Vinyl

TWO-TEN SEDANS

Combination No. 503
Dark Blue Gabardine

Light Blue Pattern Cloth

Combination No. 504
Dark Green Gabardine

Light Green Pattern Cloth

Combination No. 505
Brown Gabardine

Light Tan Pattern Cloth

TWO-TEN DELRAY CLUB COUPE

Combination No. 506

Beige Vinyl

Blue Vinyl

Combination No. 507

Beige Vinyl

Green Vinyl

Combination No. 508

Ivory Vinyl

Black Vinyl

Combination 542

Vinyl

Waffle n Vinyl

Combination No. 545

Ivory Vinyl

Turquoise Waffle Pattern Vinyl

Combination No. 543

Beige Vinyl

Brown Waffle Pattern Vinyl

Combination No. 546

Coral Vinyl

Gray Waffle Pattern Vinyl

TWO-TEN STATION WAGONS

Combination No. 514

Beige Vinyl

Blue Ribbed Vinyl

Combination No. 515
Light Green Vinyl

Dark Green Ribbed Vinyl

Combination No. 516

Beige Vinyl

Brown Ribbed Vinyl

ONE-FIFTY SEDANS

Combination No. 500

Black Vinyl

Gray Pattern Cloth

STATION WAGON

Combination No. 502

Brown Vinyl

Straw Textured Vinyl

Combination No. 524
Light Green Vinyl

Dark Green Textured Vinyl

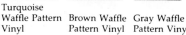

kee Avenue in Detroit. Advance Body Design had begun with thousands of preliminary sketches...boiled them down to a handful, then rendered these in full-scale side view. But the final designs just wouldn't come, and [company styling chief] Harley Earl was getting increasingly upset....[Early front-end themes] were slightly reminiscent of the [1952–53] Aero Willys, and proposed taillight designs were reaching a hopeless stage of tortured, overworked features. Suddenly, Earl blew his top, and that did wonders."

The result was largely the work of Chevy studio head Clare MacKichan, staff designer Carl H. Renner, and body engineer Charles A. Stebbins. Following Earl's dictum of "go all the way, then back off," they produced a knockout package only a bit less radical than initially envisioned. Uncommonly clean for the period, it was boxy yet altogether sleeker than the stodgy 1953–54 models despite the unchanged wheelbase.

"Longer-Lower-Wider" was Detroit's order of the day, so overall height was slashed by up to six inches on wagons and 2.5 inches on other models, aided by the new chassis' lower ride height. Oddly, the '55 was about an inch shorter and narrower overall but *looked* longer and wider, thanks to a hood almost level with the front fenders and Chevy's first fully flush rear fenders.

Only one element proved controversial: the Ferrari-like, eggcrate rectangular grille. Earl liked its simplicity, but management didn't, favoring a shinier, full-width treatment that was also in the running (and adopted for '56). Some dealers didn't like it either, finding it a tough sell against the glittering dentistry of the '55 Ford and Plymouth. But as Renner observed: "Mr. Earl possessed much power. ...And although some individuals did not agree with his decisions, being boss, he had his own way."

The '55 Chevy was unquestionably a Harley Earl design, and successfully combined a number of his favorite ideas. For example, the fashionable "Sweep Sight" wraparound windshield, also new to Chevy, dated from his 1951 LeSabre show car, the first Corvette, and the limited-edition 1953 Buick Skylark, Cadillac Eldorado, and Oldsmobile Fiesta convertibles. The last also introduced the rakish beltline dip or notch used on all models save wagons. MacKichan explained that this stemmed from Earl's fondness for low roofs. "He liked low windows [and] low rear quarters, so to get that feeling he wanted to raise the rear fender, and sometimes it was higher than the beltline....That is how we got into that kind of dipped shape." Stylists also experimented with a hood set *lower* than the front fenders, then dismissed it as ungainly. Wagons featured curved rear side glass, an innovation for this increasingly popular body type that answered growing buyer demand for less utilitarian looks.

Renner credits some of Earl's aesthetic preferences to his physical stature: "He was six-foot four, and mockups looked quite different to him than they would to an average-size person. Therefore...designers [sometimes] strapped blocks of wood to their

The '55 Chevy Bel Air convertible was offered in three solid colors and seven two-tones. Most were seen in two-tone form, such as this Gypsy Red/Shoreline Beige example (*far left*). It shows to good effect the optional grille guard and the Ferrari-like grille that was probably the car's most controversial design element. Six color combinations were available for the all-vinyl interior, red and beige being the choice here (*left*). All Bel Airs came with a three-spoke steering wheel and a bright trim panel that ran across the dash. The latter contained 987 miniature Chevy bow ties! (Owner: James R. Cahill)

shoes, which afforded them the same vantage point—all unknown to Mr. Earl, of course."

Two-toning helped sell cars in the mid-Fifties, and the new Chevy had some of the best. It was most daring on non-wagon Bel Airs. Roof, rear deck, and upper rear fenders wore one shade, with the bodyside color break defined by a horizontal chrome strip running rearward from a short "slash" molding at the beltline dip. Other models had simpler side trim, so their contrasting color was confined to the roof—until later in the model year.

Hooded headlamps were also *de rigeur*, and these were nicely blended into the new flat-top front fenders. Chuck Stebbins conceived the functional tail lamps, which jutted out slightly from the rear fenders and could thus be seen from the sides. This design was originally intended to define a prominent horizontal decklid crease just above the license plate, with the sheetmetal below set back slightly for a sculptured effect. Here, Earl and Cole were overruled—probably for cost reasons—by Harlow

Curtice, named GM president in 1953 when "Engine Charlie" Wilson left to become Secretary of Defense in the Eisenhower Administration.

"Nothing was carried over," MacKichan said later. "With the new V-8 and the young man's image. . .we tried to get it more youthful. [Yet] there *was* a Cadillac feeling. . . .Those headlight eyebrows, the eagle hood ornament [a Carl Renner contribution], the wraparound windshield. And the taillights were designed to give a Cadillac look. . . . I don't think 'copy' is the right word, but the flavor [was] definitely there."

Interior alterations were just as extensive. Soft trim, developed by Ed Donaldson, was plusher and more expensive-looking than before (especially Bel Air's new "waffle" patterned vinyl), while Renner's symmetrically arranged instrument panel was refreshingly subdued next to Chevy's recent "jukebox" dashboards. Instruments nestled directly ahead of the wheel in a simple fan-shaped cluster that was matched on the right by the radio speaker housing, the "twin-

cowl" motif introduced with the first Corvette. Bel Air panels wore a full-width appliqué embossed with tiny versions of the Chevy "bow-tie" logo—987 in all. Enhancing comfort was a new "High Level" ventilation system, via a mesh-covered air intake on the topside of the cowl.

Introduced under the "Motoramic" label, Chevrolet's 1955 lineup (see chart) initially comprised 14 models in the same three series as 1953–54. A Two-Ten Sport Coupe hardtop arrived in June 1955, while that most singular of wagons, the two-door Nomad, joined the top-line Bel Air group in February.

The Nomad is a story in itself. Significant as the first production car to combine the best design attributes of station wagon and hardtop coupe—the Fifties' two most influential body styles—it was another Harley Earl idea, though MacKichan's staff first suggested a "sport wagon" as one of two additions to the '55 line. (The other, a long-deck, three-window "Executive Coupe," never got off the drawing board.) "The Corvette theme was a popular one," MacKichan recalled, and "Carl Renner. . .had come up with a sketch for a station wagon roof that caught Earl's eye. Bringing this idea to the Chevrolet studio, Earl asked that it be incorporated into a station wagon version as one of [three] Corvette idea cars for the 1954 Motorama."

Thus was born the Corvette Nomad, a non-running exercise with fiberglass bodywork on a conventional 1953 Chevrolet station wagon chassis. Renner's roof nicely suited the lower body lines of Chevy's recently an-

Opposite page: One of the most attractive models in the mid-price Two-Ten series was the Delray Club Coupe (*top and bottom left*). With extra-cost two-toning, it looked very much like a Bel Air from the outside, although it lacked the chrome spear on the front fender and door and the Bel Air badges. Note also that the horizontal side chrome piece is not painted in the center, as on the Bel Air. However, it was the interior that set the Delray apart fom all other Chevy models. Its main feature was the attractive (and practical) two-tone all-vinyl interior. The seats were stitched into a pattern of squares, which was carried over onto the doors. Note the two-spoke steering wheel (*bottom right*).

nounced sports car, and the stylists couldn't have picked a better name. First seen in January 1954 at New York's Waldorf-Astoria Hotel, the Corvette Nomad was such a hit that Earl's assistant, Howard O'Leary, hurriedly called MacKichan and ordered its roof styling adapted for the new standard Chevrolet—giving him just two days to do it.

Renner hustled. "The [show car's] roof was taken from a full-size drawing, cut apart, stretched out, and mated to the...1955 Chevrolet lower body," said MacKichan. "The hardtop front-door glass framing, forward-

sloping rear quarters, wide B-pillar, fluted roof, wraparound rear side glass, the rear wheel housing cutout, and the seven vertical accent strips on the tailgate [later nicknamed "bananas" by enthusiasts] were all retained in a remarkably good translation from the dream car." Aside from all-steel bodywork, the production Bel Air Nomad differed in using a conventional liftgate—a heavy, chrome-plated die-cast affair—instead of the show car's drop-down tailgate window. The "fluted roof" refers to nine transverse grooves at the rear, a visual remnant of Earl's plan for a

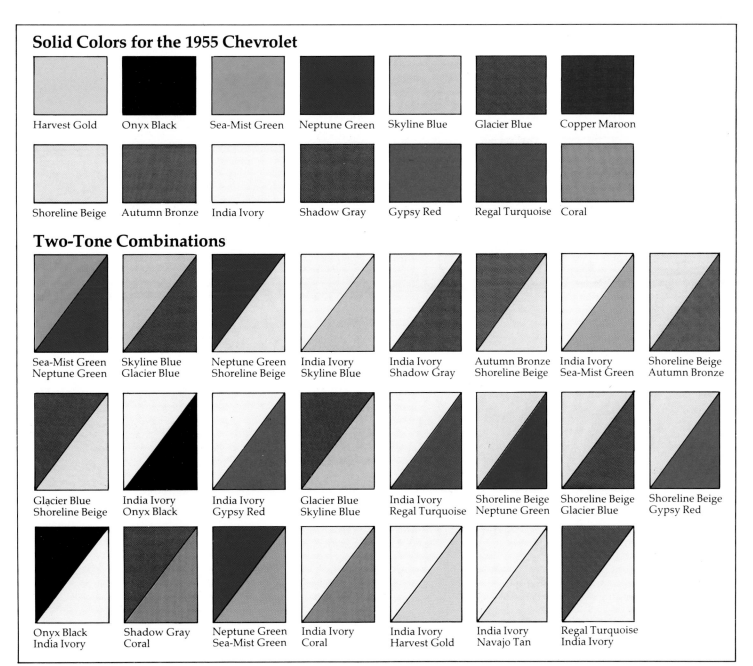

Solid Colors for the 1955 Chevrolet

Harvest Gold | Onyx Black | Sea-Mist Green | Neptune Green | Skyline Blue | Glacier Blue | Copper Maroon

Shoreline Beige | Autumn Bronze | India Ivory | Shadow Gray | Gypsy Red | Regal Turquoise | Coral

Two-Tone Combinations

Sea-Mist Green / Neptune Green | Skyline Blue / Glacier Blue | Neptune Green / Shoreline Beige | India Ivory / Skyline Blue | India Ivory / Shadow Gray | Autumn Bronze / Shoreline Beige | India Ivory / Sea-Mist Green | Shoreline Beige / Autumn Bronze

Glacier Blue / Shoreline Beige | India Ivory / Onyx Black | India Ivory / Gypsy Red | Glacier Blue / Skyline Blue | India Ivory / Regal Turquoise | Shoreline Beige / Neptune Green | Shoreline Beige / Glacier Blue | Shoreline Beige / Gypsy Red

Onyx Black / India Ivory | Shadow Gray / Coral | Neptune Green / Sea-Mist Green | India Ivory / Coral | India Ivory / Harvest Gold | India Ivory / Navajo Tan | Regal Turquoise / India Ivory

At $2571, Nomad (*top*) was the priciest model in Chevrolet's '55 lineup; it was also the least bought. Today, however, it is probably the most sought after '55 Chevy. It took its styling cues from the 1954 Chevrolet Nomad (*both photos, middle row*), a Corvette-based show car that made the rounds at GM's Motorama. The photo of this Nomad (*bottom left*) was shot on March 11, 1954; except for trim, it appears production-ready. Chevy designers were tinkering with roof lines and wheel openings in early 1955 (*bottom right*).

telescoping stainless-steel section that was quickly precluded by leak worries and high cost.

Pontiac got a Nomad too, the Safari, but only at the last minute and over Chevrolet's objections. Alas, the marriage of hardtop flair and wagon utility wasn't bliss in either version. Though it looked like other '55 Chevys, the Nomad shared little with them aft of the cowl and was thus the most expensive

Chevy ever: $2571 with V-8—$265 more than a similarly equipped Bel Air convertible. The lack of four doors also limited its appeal, especially among wagon buyers. Then too, the glassy interior was great for visibility but uncomfortably warm on sunny days, the liftgate sucked in exhaust fumes when open, and the slanted rear was prone to water leaks. With all this, the Nomad was Chevy's least popular '55,

Exterior Color Selections for the 1955 Chevrolet

1955 COLORS	Bel-Air 4-door sedan	Bel-Air 2-door sedan	Bel-Air Sport Coupe	Bel-Air Convertible	Bel-Air Station Wagon	Bel-Air Nomad	Two-Ten 4-door sedan	Two-Ten 2-door sedan	Two-Ten Sport Coupe	Two-Ten Delray Club Coupe	Two-Ten 2-door Station Wagon	Two-Ten 4-door Station Wagon	One-Fifty 4-door sedan	One-Fifty 2-door sedan	One-Fifty Utility sedan	One-Fifty 2-door Station Wagon
SOLID COLORS																
Harvest Gold			●													
Onyx Black	●	●	●	●			●	●		●			●	●	●	
Sea-Mist Green	●	●					●	●		●			●	●	●	●
Neptune Green	●	●	●		●		●	●		●	●	●	●	●	●	●
Skyline Blue	●	●					●	●		●			●	●		
Glacier Blue	●	●	●		●		●	●		●	●	●	●	●		
Copper Maroon		●	●				●	●					●	●		
Shoreline Beige	●	●	●		●	●					●	●	●	●		
Autumn Bronze							●	●			●	●	●	●	●	●
India Ivory	●	●					●	●		●			●	●	●	
Shadow Gray	●	●					●	●					●	●		
Gypsy Red				●												
Regal Turquoise					●											
Coral				●												
TWO-TONE																
Sea-Mist Green / Neptune Green	●	●					●	●			●	●	●	●	●	●
Skyline Blue / Glacier Blue	●	●					●	●					●	●	●	
Neptune Green / Shoreline Beige			●													
India Ivory / Skyline Blue	●	●	●				●	●		●			●	●	●	
India Ivory / Shadow Gray	●	●				●	●						●	●	●	
Autumn Bronze / Shoreline Beige											●	●				
India Ivory / Sea-Mist Green							●	●		●						
Shoreline Beige / Autumn Bronze	●	●		●	●	●	●	●								●
Glacier Blue / Shoreline Beige							●	●		●						
India Ivory / Onyx Black										●						
India Ivory / Gypsy Red						●				●						
Glacier Blue / Skyline Blue				●							●	●				
India Ivory / Regal Turquoise	●	●	●	●		●										
Shoreline Beige / Neptune Green	●	●	●				●	●					●	●	●	
Shoreline Beige / Glacier Blue			●		●	●					●	●				
Shoreline Beige / Gypsy Red			●		●	●										
Onyx Black / India Ivory										●						
Shadow Gray / Coral	●	●	●			●										
Neptune Green / Sea-Mist Green					●	●					●					
India Ivory / Coral				●												
India Ivory / Harvest Gold	●	●	●	●		●				●						
India Ivory / Navajo Tan						●										
Regal Turquoise / India Ivory						●										

23

One of the most overlooked models offered by Chevy in 1955 was the Two-Ten Sport Coupe (*above*). Buyers largely ignored it at the time, so it's difficult to find one now. Production amounted to only 11,675 units, compared to 185,562 for the more expensive Bel Air hardtop. However, since the price difference amounted to less than $150, most customers probably felt the extra money was well spent. After all, the Bel Air sported more exterior chrome, a flashier interior, and more standard equipment.

garnering only 8386 orders. Of course, it's long been the most collectible for that very reason, as well as its handsome looks—and the fact that it's a '55 Chevy.

Chevrolet 1955 was greeted with near universal acclaim. *Mechanix Illustrated* magazine's veteran tester Tom McCahill called it "a junior-size Olds with Buick doors and a Cadillac rear, the most glamorous-looking and

hottest-performing Chevy to come down the pike...rugged competition for Ford in the scramble to see which American car will outsell all others."

While performance was expected from the new V-8, fine roadability was a pleasant surprise. "Best-handling Chevrolet I have ever driven," reported Floyd Clymer in *Popular Mechanics*, "and it feels like a large car." *Motor Trend*'s editors named Chevy (and the '55 Mercury) the year's top handler. Said Walt Woron: "That mushy feeling, so long associated with the American automobile, is gone. In its place is...solid sureness, a willingness to be steered, not aimed [and his car didn't have power assist]. ...When we deliberately drove it off the shoulder, [it] wouldn't whip so as to cause us to lose control. ...We could throw it into turns at practically any speed, [even those] that would make other cars quail."

Criticisms were surprisingly few for mass-production cars. Ride was generally judged a bit hard, while *Road & Track* magazine found the steering woefully slow at 4.5 turns lock-to-lock, and felt handling had "plenty of room for improvement." Some testers de-

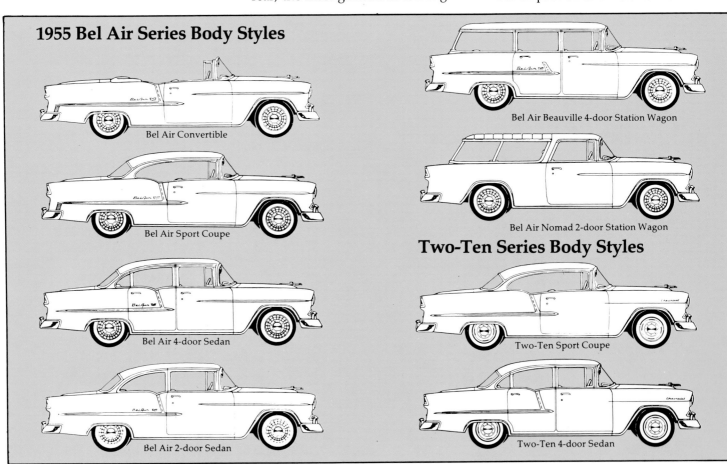

1955 Bel Air Series Body Styles

Bel Air Convertible

Bel Air Sport Coupe

Bel Air 4-door Sedan

Bel Air 2-door Sedan

Bel Air Beauville 4-door Station Wagon

Bel Air Nomad 2-door Station Wagon

Two-Ten Series Body Styles

Two-Ten Sport Coupe

Two-Ten 4-door Sedan

plored the switch from gauges to warning lights for oil pressure and generator, while others found seat travel insufficient and the steering wheel too high and close.

But such quibbles were easily overshadowed by styling that most everybody liked and V-8 go that had everybody talking. The "old man's" car was dead: long live "The Hot One!" Even in basic, 162-bhp form, the 265 was both stronger and thriftier than Plymouth's new 260 V-8 or Ford's enlarged, 262 Y-block—and it had less weight to haul.

The figures told the story. Clymer's Powerglide-equipped Bel Air topped 108 mph, while *Motor Trend*'s 180-bhp car did 0–60 mph in 11.4 seconds (in Low range), the standing quarter-mile in 18.4 seconds, and the 50–80 mph spurt (with Low held to 60 mph) in 12.9 seconds. *Road & Track* got the best numbers by ordering the stick-overdrive/Power Pack combo in a light Two-Ten two-door: 9.7 seconds 0–60 mph, 17.2 seconds in the standing quarter-mile. Fuel economy? A creditable 18–22 miles per gallon.

Such formidable performance inevitably led to competition, beginning with the Daytona Speed Weeks in February. Jack Radtke finished 10th overall in the traditional road-and-beach race against Buicks, Oldsmobiles, and Chrysler 300s, while other Chevys took the top four spots in class and eight of the first 11 positions. In the two-way measured mile, three more Chevys were among the five fastest cars with engines of 250–299 cid. Soon, "Smokey" Yunick entered a V-8 Chevy in National Association for Stock Car Automobile Racing short-track contests, where it proved unbeatable in the hands of former Hudson pilot Herb Thomas. It was equally capable in NASCAR's longer Grand National events, with Thomas and Fonty Flock often winning against much larger and more powerful machinery.

Observing these early exploits, Ed Cole began issuing certain heavy-duty "export" parts through dealers, a ploy other makes were using to get their best hardware into racers' hands. It paid off. Thomas won the Southern 500 at Darlington, South Carolina on Labor Day at an average 92.281 mph, followed by Jim Reed in another Chevy. Tim Flock, Fonty's brother, was third in a Chrysler 300, but

Chevys also finished 4th, 7th, and 8 through 10—*seven* of the first 10 finishers. October brought a repeat performance at Charlotte, and Chevy ran 1-2 at Atlanta. Meanwhile, another ex-Hudson driver, Marshall Teague, began dominating the American Automobile Association circuit. Symbolizing Chevy's new performance prowess, a Bel Air convertible was selected as pace car for the year's Indy 500. In all, 1955 was the greatest competition year for a low-price make in recent memory.

It was certainly a great year for Chevy buyers, who could now personalize their cars more than ever. Air conditioning was the most expensive extra at $565—and thus not often ordered—but others were downright cheap. The base V-8, for example, cost a mere $99, overdrive added $108, power steering $92, and "Pivot Pedal" power brakes just $38. Also available were a $123 "wheel carrier continental," manual-tune and Custom signal-seeking radios, recirculating heater/defroster, DeLuxe heater, windshield washer, electric clock, parking brake warning lamp, full wheel covers, and the usual chrome exterior embellish-

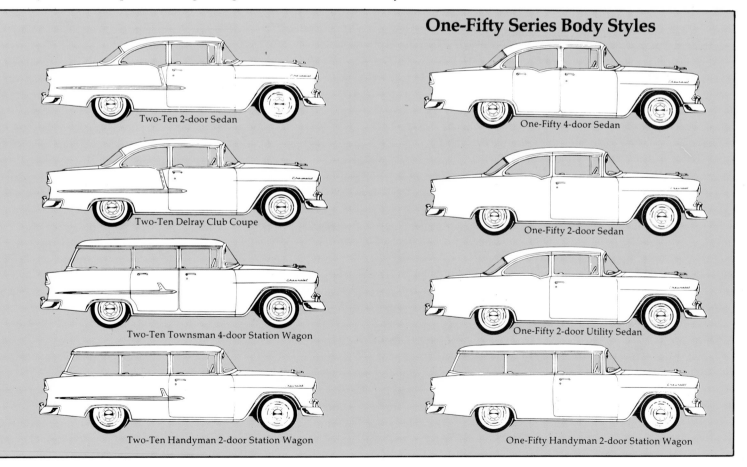

One-Fifty Series Body Styles

Two-Ten 2-door Sedan

Two-Ten Delray Club Coupe

Two-Ten Townsman 4-door Station Wagon

Two-Ten Handyman 2-door Station Wagon

One-Fifty 4-door Sedan

One-Fifty 2-door Sedan

One-Fifty 2-door Utility Sedan

One-Fifty Handyman 2-door Station Wagon

General Motors, the automotive colossus, built its 50-millionth car on November 23, 1954. It was entirely fitting that it should be an all-gold 1955 Chevrolet Bel Air Sport Coupe (*right*). In addition to a "fitting ceremony" at the assembly plant (*left*), civic luncheons were held in 65 cities from coast to coast and GM plants across the country held open house to more than a million people.

ments: grille guard, body sill moldings, exhaust extensions, side window ventshades, and shields for fenders, door handles, and gas filler flap. Interior extras included floormats, accelerator pedal cover, chrome-plated tissue dispenser, compass, a "Glamour Glide" front seat cushion protector of "rich nylon-dacron," luggage compartment lamp, portable underhood spotlight, and a "four-contour" GM electric shaver "for use in car or home."

But the most interesting item in Chevy's 1955 color, trim, and accessories book is the one that didn't actually appear for another three years—and then only on a Cadillac. This was the "Automatic Top Raiser," a typically Fifties gadget that Harley Earl had been playing with on various show cars for some time. Described as "a new, modern electronic device that will automatically raise a convertible's top at the first drops of rain when the car is unattended," it was subsequently withdrawn, no doubt due to technical problems. The only time it saw "production" was when Cadillac used it on five mildly modified 1958 Eldorado Biarritz convertibles built for that year's auto show season.

In retrospect, the 1955 Chevrolet was a stunning achievement that marked a turning point for "USA-1." Seldom had a mass-market Detroiter been so completely transformed in one year—or so successfully. All of a sudden, a name once synonymous with dull but durable low-price transportation had a bright new luster of youthful zest, sizzling performance, and race-proved stamina. And despite stronger-than-ever competition, Chevy solidified its position as industry sales leader, beating Ford by some 250,000 units in model year production and by nearly 66,000 for the calendar year.

Only one question remained: what would Chevy do for an encore?

1955
Accessories

Fender antenna	Outside rearview mirrors
Self deicing wiper blade	Inside non-glare rearview mirror
Wiring junction block	Vanity visor
Power brakes	Body sill molding
Locking gas cap	Radio: manual, push-button, or
Continental wheel carrier	signal-seeking
Electric clock	Automatic top raiser (convertible)
Compass	Arm rests
Nylon/plastic/fiber seat covers	Wheel trim rings
Accelerator pedal cover	Safetylight with mirror
Wheel covers	Power-positioned front seat
Wire wheel covers	Electric shaver
Tissue dispenser	Parking brake signal
Exhaust extension	Door handle shields
Oil filter and element	Front fender shields
License plate frame	Rear seat speaker
Glareshades	Spotlamp
Grille guard	Power steering
Fender guard	Whitewall tires
Door edge guard	Ventshades
Gasoline filler guard	Outside visors
Heater and defroster	Inside visors
Tool kit	Traffic light viewer
Back-up lamps	Windshield washer (vacuum or
Courtesy lamps	foot-operated)
Cigarette lighter	Electric-power window lifts
Floor mats	

1955 Chevrolet Specifications, Prices, and Production

Model	Overall Length	Curb Weight	List Price	Production
1955 (115-inch wheelbase)				
ONE-FIFTY				
1502 Sedan, two-door	195.6	3,145	1,685	99,146
1503 Sedan, four-door	195.6	3,150	1,728	29,898
1512 Sedan, utility	195.6	3,070	1,593	11,196
1529 Handyman, two-door wagon	197.1	3,275	2,030	17,936
TWO-TEN				
2102 Sedan, two-door	195.6	3,130	1,775	249,105
2103 Sedan, four-door	195.6	3,165	1,819	317,724
2109 Townsman, four-door wagon	197.1	3,335	2,127	82,303
2124 Delray, coupe	195.6	3,130	1,835	115,584
2129 Handyman, two-door wagon	197.1	3,315	2,079	28,918
2154 Hardtop, coupe	195.6	3,155	1,959	11,675
BEL AIR				
2402 Sedan, two-door	195.6	3,140	1,888	168,313
2403 Sedan, four-door	195.6	3,185	1,932	345,372
2409 Beauville, four-door wagon	197.1	3,370	2,262	24,313
2429 Nomad, two-door wagon	197.1	3,285	2,472	8,386
2434 Convertible, coupe	195.6	3,300	2,206	41,292
2454 Sport Coupe, hardtop	195.6	3,180	2,067	185,562

Engine/Transmission Availability

	cid	bore/stroke (inches)	compression ratio	bhp @ rpm	carb	trans
1955						
Six	235	3.56 × 3.94	7.5:1	123 @ 3800	1V	3-sp., OD
Six	235	3.56 × 3.94	7.5:1	136 @ 4200	1V	PG[1]
V-8	265	3.75 × 3.00	8.0:1	162 @ 4400	2V	3-sp., OD, PG[1]
V-8	265	3.75 × 3.00	8.0:1	180 @ 4600	4V	3-sp., OD, PG[1]

[1]Powerglide

1956:
"Loves to Go . . . And Looks It!"

Ads for the '56 Chevy proclaimed that "The Hot One's Even Hotter." And it was, with up to 225 horsepower. Updated styling featured a bold, full-width grille and a bulkier, more important look. "USA-1," of course, remained exactly that.

Above: 1956 Bel Air convertible. (Owner: Gary Johns)

Middle children tend to be ignored in many families, and the 1956 Chevrolet is no exception. Though revered as a "classic" Chevy, it's long been eclipsed in enthusiast affections by the trail-blazing '55 and the speedier, shinier '57. That's unfortunate. In many ways, the '56 is the best of both worlds: faster and flashier than its predecessor, yet closer than its successor to the lithe simplicity of Ed Cole's original concept.

It was certainly the most successful "classic" Chevy in commercial terms, a fact largely ignored. Despite a broad sales retreat, Detroit built nearly 6.3 million cars for model year '56. Chevrolet claimed no less than 44 percent of low-price sales as its total market share rose from 23 percent (which was actually down 2.5 points on '54) to 27.9 percent, the highest of the three "classic" years. Remarkably, Chevy managed this on just 88 percent of its 1955 volume. By contrast, Ford fell to 77 percent of its previous ouptut and Plymouth plunged to 60 percent. (The latter undoubtedly helped Dearborn grab a 23.7-percent slice of the industry pie, up 1.5 percent from '55.)

The car that worked these wonders could be easily dismissed as a warmed-up '55—which it mostly *was*—though that was hardly bad, considering what Chevrolet had to warm up. Besides, conventional design wisdom in mid-Fifties Detroit was that to sell well, a car had to *look* new even if it wasn't—particularly if it was a ground-up-fresh design from the year before. Industry critics called this "planned obsolescence."

Mastering that art well before anyone else had helped General Motors achieve industry dominance by the early Fifties. So there was no question that the '56 Chevrolet would be as visually different from the '55 as possible, albeit within the monetary bounds of Detroit's then-customary three-year life cycle of new design/minor facelift/major facelift. Still, the sums lavished on the '56 Chevy were extravagant even for this free-spending decade. The restyle alone cost no less than $40 million, with $1 million just for the front fenders!

Of course, there *was* a reason. Chevrolet began '56 planning before its '55 debuted, and some division managers were likely nervous about public reaction to such a radically different Chevy. They needn't have worried, as we know now, but they didn't have the benefit of hindsight. All they knew in early 1954 was that they were locked into this design for three years, and if buyers didn't go for it in '55, recovery would hinge on the changes made for '56.

This thinking shaped the in-between "classic" Chevy as much as contemporary market trends, which increasingly favored bigger, brighter cars with more horsepower and better performance. The '56 complied.

According to Chevy studio chief Clare MacKichan, the '56 styling brief called for a more "imposing" front end "and a little more chrome on the sides" than the '55. But by the time his staff had finished, they'd changed all sheetmetal below the beltline save the doors. The result was even more like Cadillac than the '55: bulkier, though not heavy-looking. In fact, it was one of the era's better facelifts, relatively conservative and astutely executed.

Specifically, the '55's small, understated grille gave way to a shiny full-width latticework incorporating a large, square parking lamp at each end. Above was a flatter, four-inch-longer hood bearing a large Chevy emblem, a wide chrome "V" on V-8

Opposite page: Clay mock-ups for the 1956 Chevy—all from May 1954—indicate that the taillight design was decided early on. Note that all of these studies feature a large rear wheel opening similar to the 1955 Nomad, but which did not make it to production on the 1956 models, Nomad included. Two cars (*center and bottom left*) sport variations of 1953–54 Bel Air rear fender trim. *This page:* Side trim (*top and bottom rows*) intended for the '56 Bel Air actually ended up on the One-Fifty series. Grille design started out as an exaggerated '55 (*top and center left*), but by October, 1954 had evolved into the production version (*center and bottom right*). One grille (*opposite page, top left*) actually predicted the '57 front end. Verical headlight pods (*both pages*) also received serious consideration.

models, and a new stylized jet plane ornament. Front fenders were broader, headlamp eyebrows reshaped to suit, and a larger front bumper appeared with a slight central "vee," echoing hoodfront contour.

Along the flanks, wheel openings were rakishly flared, and L-shaped side trim dressed up the previously bare One-Fifty models, allowing them to be ordered with optional two-tone bodyside paint for the first time. Two-

Tens and Bel Airs wore more elaborate moldings that gave them bolder two-toning than in '55.

Bringing up the rear were extended fenders with large, chrome-plated clusters nestling in vertically cut notches. Each housed (extra-cost) a rectangular backup lamp between a conical tail lamp above and a small, round reflector in a bullet-shaped pod below. The left unit opened from the top to reveal a newly hidden fuel filler

à la Cadillac. Though Chevrolet resisted the finny uplifts of this year's Plymouth and Dodge, its '56 tail had the same general air. A deeper-section back bumper provided the finishing touch.

Overall, the '56 was busier than the '55 but more in tune with the times. Of course, GM design chief Harley Earl knew saleable styling better than anyone. Was he now having second thoughts about the '55? "Very possi-

33

Right, both pages: Nomad received the same facelift for '56 as other Chevrolets, including the rear-wheel cutouts, but retained its unique look. At $2608 it was the year's priciest, and the rarest, too, with only 7886 built. (Owner: Ron Pittman)

bly," as MacKichan told *COLLECT-IBLE AUTOMOBILE®* magazine. "Whatever ideas people had when the '56 was being done were carryovers from when the '55 was done [and] Earl finally agreed that maybe the bigger grille would be alright for the '56....I think his mind was changing at the time, though some of his earlier cars had quite a lot of chrome on the sides. Many times I heard him remark that you need 'entertainment' on the side of a car."

Though width, height, and wheelbase stayed the same, the '56's fore and aft revisions added 2–3 inches in overall length for a total of 200.8 inches on wagons and 197.5 on other body styles. Together with the new side trim, they made appearance more streamlined. Interior dimensions and the basic '55 instrument panel weren't changed either, but there were the usual new colors and upholstery materials, and rectangular slots replaced the myriad of "bow ties" on the Bel Air

dash appliqué.

Chevy's '56 lineup (see chart) was as much in tune with the times as its styling. The three familiar series now spanned 19 models—three more than '55—plus 12 powerteams, 10 solid colors, and 14 two-tone combinations. Included was a new body style, the four-door hardtop, a GM first from 1955 (at Buick and Olds) adopted by most other makes this year. Called Sport Sedan and available in both Two-

Ten and Bel Air versions, it was advertised as "embodying the youthful lines of a convertible, the practicality of a hardtop, and the convenience of a sedan." With wagon sales rising, Chevy switched the Bel Air Beauville from six- to nine-passenger seating and issued a Two-Ten counterpart, bringing wagon offerings to six. Other models were continued from '55.

The swanky Nomad wagon bowed with the rest of the line this time, and

Interior Color and Trim Selections for the 1956 Chevrolet

BEL AIR CONVERTIBLE

Combination No. 602
Ivory Vinyl

Charcoal Gray Pattern Vinyl

Combination No. 621
Tan Vinyl
Copper Pattern Vinyl

BEL AIR BEAUVILLE/NOMAD STATION WAGONS

Combination No. 610/611
Ivory Vinyl

Charcoal Gray Pattern Cloth

Combination No. 619/620
Copper Vinyl
Tan Pattern Cloth

BEL AIR CONVERTIBLE (CUSTOM-COLORED INTERIORS)

Combination No. 607
Light Blue Vinyl
Dark Blue Pattern Vinyl

Combination No. 605
Ivory Vinyl

Red Pattern Vinyl

Combination No. 603
Ivory Vinyl

Dark Turquoise Pattern Vinyl

Combination No. 604
Yellow Vinyl

Charcoal Gray Pattern Vinyl

Combination No. 606
Light Green Vinyl

Dark Green Pattern Vinyl

BEL AIR SPORT SEDAN AND SPORT COUPE (CUSTOM-COLORED INTERIORS)

Combination No. 580
Light Green Vinyl

Dark Green Pattern Cloth

Combination No. 584
Light Turquoise Vinyl
Dark Turquoise Pattern Cloth

Combination No. 581
Light Blue Vinyl

Dark Blue Pattern Cloth

Combination No. 585
Yellow Vinyl

Charcoal Gray Pattern Cloth

Combination No. 583
Red Vinyl

Beige Pattern Cloth

BEL AIR SEDANS

Combination No. 573
Ivory Vinyl

Charcoal Gray Pattern Cloth

Combination No. 617
Tan Vinyl
Copper Pattern Cloth

BEL AIR SPORT SEDAN AND SPORT COUPE

Combination No. 579
Ivory Vinyl

Charcoal Gray Pattern Cloth

Combination No. 618
Copper Vinyl
Tan Pattern Cloth

Beauville, replacing the previous "waffle" material, and all exterior trim was now stock Bel Air save the sparkling tailgate "bananas" and, unique to the '56, a small chrome "V" below each tail lamp (other Chevys signified a V-8 with one large "V" on trunklid or tailgate). A nice detail touch was reversing the Bel Air's short rear-quarter "slash" moldings to match the angle of the slanted B-pillars. Alas, base price rose more than $130, to $2608 with six, and production declined to 7886 units, about .5 percent of Chevy's total '56 volume.

Chevy hoped that a full year would push sales past the 10,000 mark. *Motor Trend* named it one of the year's most beautiful cars while admitting that "its distinct personal-car feel forces certain limiting features...the low roofline, compact overall package, sharply sloping rear." Yet former GM stylist Pierre Ollier disputes the myth that "Nomads traded off interior space for sporty looks....Nomad had more cargo capacity with the second seat up than the 1955 Buick, Studebaker, Rambler, and several other contemporary wagons. With its rear seat [folded, it] had a longer cargo floor than 1955 Dodge, Ford, Plymouth, Rambler, and Stude wagons."

Nevertheless, Nomad still suffered from having just two doors instead of four—and a high price. The latter prompted a bit of cost-cutting this year. Seat inserts were borrowed from standard Bel Air hardtops and the

With the "horsepower race" more important than ever in the sales race, Chevy couldn't afford to rest on its '55 laurels, so performance again vied with styling for customer attention in '56. "The Hot One's Even Hotter," said one ad. "Loves to Go...And Looks It!" said another. Chevy served notice even before the '56s went on sale. On Labor Day 1955, a heavily disguised Bel Air Sport Sedan charged up Pikes Peak in 17 minutes, 24.05 seconds to set a new American stock-sedan record—fully two minutes, three seconds faster than the previous best.

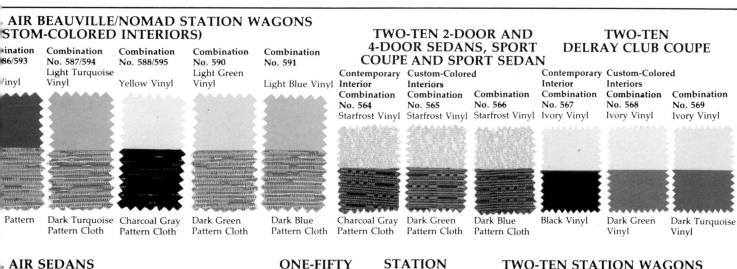

AIR BEAUVILLE/NOMAD STATION WAGONS (STOM-COLORED INTERIORS) / TWO-TEN 2-DOOR AND 4-DOOR SEDANS, SPORT COUPE AND SPORT SEDAN / TWO-TEN DELRAY CLUB COUPE

AIR SEDANS (STOM-COLORED INTERIORS) / ONE-FIFTY SEDANS / STATION WAGON / TWO-TEN STATION WAGONS

1956 COLORS	Bel-Air			
	2-door Sedan	4-door Sedan	Sport Sedan	
SOLID COLORS				
Onyx Black	●	●	●	
Pinecrest Green	●	●	●	
Sherwood Green	●	●	●	
Nassau Blue	●	●	●	
Harbor Blue	●	●	●	
Dusk Plum	●	●	●	
India Ivory	●	●	●	
Matador Red	●	●	●	
Twilight Turquoise	●	●	●	
Crocus Yellow	●	●	●	
TWO-TONE				
India Ivory Onyx Black	●	●	●	
Sherwood Green Pinecrest Green	●	●	●	
India Ivory Sherwood Green	●	●	●	
India Ivory Pinecrest Green	●	●	●	
Crocus Yellow Laurel Green	●	●	●	
Nassau Blue Harbor Blue	●	●	●	
India Ivory Nassau Blue	●	●	●	
India Ivory Dusk Plum	●	●	●	
Adobe Beige Sierra Gold	●	●	●	
India Ivory Dawn Gray	●	●	●	
Onyx Black Crocus Yellow	●	●	●	
India Ivory Matador Red	●	●		
Dune Beige Matador Red			●	
India Ivory Twilight Turquoise	●	●	●	

Convertible Top Colors: I-Ivory; B-Blue; S-Black; T-Tan

Third most popular Bel Air for 1956 was the two-door sedan (*top and center*), which beat out the Sport Coupe in the production race by a mere 1247 units. It sold for $2025 and weighed in at 3187 pounds. (Owner: Eugene R. Siuda, Jr.) The two-door hardtop, or Sport Coupe (*bottom*), cost $205 more, a penalty of about 10 percent, but added only 35 pounds of heft. Either could be equipped with the full range of options, including the most potent V-8.

Exterior Color Selections for the 1956 Chevrolet

Sport Coupe	Convertible	Beauville 9-pass. Wagon	Nomad	Two-Ten 2-door Sedan	4-door Sedan	Sport Sedan	Sport Coupe	Delray Club Coupe	Beauville 9-pass. Wagon	Townsman 4-door Wagon	Handyman 2-door Wagon	One-Fifty 2-door Sedan	4-door Sedan	Utility Sedan	Handyman 2-door Wagon
●	I,S	●	●	●	●	●	●	●	●	●	●	●	●	●	●
●	I,S,T	●		●	●	●	●	●	●	●	●	●	●	●	●
●	I,T			●	●	●	●	●	●	●	●	●	●	●	●
●	I,B,T	●		●	●	●	●	●	●	●	●	●	●	●	●
●	I,B,T			●	●	●	●	●							
●	I,T	●		●	●	●	●	●							
●	I,S	●		●	●	●	●	●	●	●	●	●	●	●	●
●	I,S	●		●	●	●	●	●	●	●	●	●	●	●	
●	I,S,T	●		●	●	●	●	●	●	●	●	●	●	●	
●	I,S	●		●	●	●	●	●	●	●	●	●	●	●	●
●	I,S	●	●	●	●	●	●	●	●	●	●	●	●	●	●
●			●	●	●	●	●	●	●	●	●	●	●	●	●
●	I,S		●	●	●	●	●	●	●	●	●				●
●	I,S	●	●	●	●	●	●	●	●	●	●	●	●	●	●
●	I,S	●	●	●	●	●	●	●	●	●	●				
●	I,B		●	●	●	●	●								
●	I,B	●	●	●	●	●	●	●	●	●	●	●	●	●	●
●	I,S	●	●	●	●	●	●	●	●	●	●				
●	T,S	●	●												
●	I,S	●	●	●	●	●	●		●	●	●				
●	I,S	●	●	●	●	●	●	●	●	●	●	●	●	●	●
	I,S			●	●	●	●	●	●	●	●	●	●	●	
●		●	●												
●	I,S	●	●	●	●	●	●	●	●	●	●				

Two-Ten and One-Fifty series available in either "Conventional Two-Toning" (top one color, body another color), or in "Special Two-Toning" (top and part of body one color, remainder of body another color).

Driven and prepared by Corvette engineering wizard Zora Arkus-Duntov, this car was powered by the new "Super Turbo-Fire" V-8, available at extra cost on any '56 Chevy. Basically, it was the existing 265 with a special "Power Pack" kit comprising specific intake manifold, higher-lift camshaft, dual exhausts, four-barrel carburetor, and 9.25:1 compression, Chevy's tightest squeeze yet. Output was a thrilling 205 horsepower at 4600 rpm and 234 pounds-feet peak torque at the same crank speed, both 14 percent above the most potent '55 powerplant's.

But it was only the beginning. Ford upped the power ante at mid-model year, so Chevy made the top Corvette engine an across-the-board passenger-car option. With mechanical instead of hydraulic lifters—the first of the famous "Duntov" cams—plus twin four-barrel carbs, lightweight valves, and larger intake and exhaust passages, it belted out 225 bhp at 5200 rpm.

Tighter 8.0:1 compression made other Chevy V-8s more potent for '56, and wilder cam profiles were ordained for all engines but the two-barrel, 162-bhp mill, which was unchanged but limited to manual transmission. The base Powerglide V-8 now produced 170 bhp at 4400 rpm and a healthy 247 lbs/ft torque at 3300 rpm. All V-8s could be ordered with full-flow (instead of bypass-type) oil filters at extra cost, thanks to minor changes in block casting and oil pan, and a reshaped gas tank allowed wagons to be equipped with dual exhausts, which had longer mufflers and shorter exhaust pipes than the '55 setup to reduce noise. Warm-up and driveability were improved via revised automatic choke (actually a mid-1955 running change), larger passages for the intake manifold heat riser, and a more deeply grooved throttle body on four-barrel carburetors. Other tweaks included "hotter" four-rib spark plugs and a beefier clutch for Super Turbo-Fire cars, with woven instead of asbestos

Opposite page: Exactly 41,268 ragtop lovers lined up to buy a '56 Bel Air, this one with optional wire-wheel covers (*top and center*). The instrument panel (*bottom left*) continued the twin-cowl, fan-shaped nacelles from 1955, but the trim strip exchanged the miniature bow ties for small rectangles. The gas cap was hidden behind the left taillight (*bottom right*). (Owner: Gary Johns)

lining, coil instead of diaphragm pressure-plate spring, and newly vented plate cover.

The old six wasn't ignored either. Now called "Blue Flame 140," it offered that many horses courtesy of 8.0:1 compression, and the hydraulic lifters previously reserved for Powerglide cars were extended to manual models. Rated torque was up to 210 lbs/ft at 4200 rpm.

To match its more muscular '56 engines, Chevy made several detail chassis revisions in apparent response to '55 criticisms. Longer, lower-rate coil springs appeared up front to reduce

nosedive in hard braking, and caster angle was increased one degree for easier steering. The rear leaf springs were mounted two inches further outboard for better cornering stability, and got wider hangers with more rubber to better resist compression from lateral axle motion. Six-leaf (instead of five-leaf) springs were a new option for all models and standard for Bel Air Beauville.

These changes were evidently effective, for the '56 Chevy got even better roadability marks than the '55. *Motor Trend's* Jim Lodge rated overall braking as very good, and lauded the

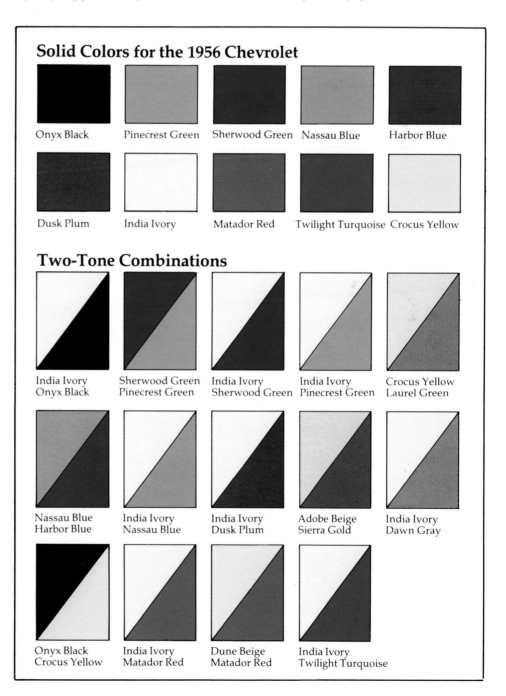

Solid Colors for the 1956 Chevrolet

Onyx Black | Pinecrest Green | Sherwood Green | Nassau Blue | Harbor Blue

Dusk Plum | India Ivory | Matador Red | Twilight Turquoise | Crocus Yellow

Two-Tone Combinations

India Ivory Onyx Black | Sherwood Green Pinecrest Green | India Ivory Sherwood Green | India Ivory Pinecrest Green | Crocus Yellow Laurel Green

Nassau Blue Harbor Blue | India Ivory Nassau Blue | India Ivory Dusk Plum | Adobe Beige Sierra Gold | India Ivory Dawn Gray

Onyx Black Crocus Yellow | India Ivory Matador Red | Dune Beige Matador Red | India Ivory Twilight Turquoise

"absence of nosedive under all stopping conditions, including panic stops." Handling earned equal praise: "Not only do we admire the steering ease of [the manual system] but believe you will be surprised to find that [the] power steering isn't as noticeable as you might think....Not many things can upset Chevy's composure on the road; it weathers normal rigors with ease. Only when it's bounced hard by a bump, or rocked into a chuckhole in the midst of a fast turn does it betray its relatively light weight and semi-stiff suspension and skip from its initial track....Recovery from bumps, dips, and potholes is rapid, non-jarring in most cases, and free from wallowing or pitching."

Alas, ride still wasn't the best, though *MT* judged it good. "Not on the soft side, [it] benefits from the car's inherent stability—that is, passengers aren't pitched or rocked from side to side on twisting roads, or see-sawed back and forth in stop-and-go driving. Seats aren't soft either, but they soak up a great deal of chassis movement, level out most minor disturbances."

Not everyone agreed with these assessments. Some testers thought ride was still too hard, and the drum brakes, though good by mid-Fifties standards, wouldn't pass muster today. Other '55 complaints —disappointing interior space, hemmed-in driving position, too few instruments, the manual's clunky column shift—were heard again in '56.

Nobody complained about performance. The basic 170 bhp/Powerglide combo returned 0–60 mph in 11.9 seconds and topped 98 mph for *Motor Life* testers, while the 205-bhp version recorded 8.9 seconds and 108.7 mph. *Motor Trend* also tried a 205-bhp/Powerglide car and got 10.7 seconds, 109.1 mph flat out, and an 18.3-second standing quarter-mile at 76 mph. Again ordering a lightweight Two-Ten two-door, *Road & Track* teamed the 205-bhp V-8 with stickshift. The results: 0–60 mph in 9 seconds flat, 111 mph top speed, and 16.6 seconds at 80 mph in the standing quarter. That was with the stock rear axle, still 3.70:1. Also as before, overdrive cars pulled 4.11:1, and those with Powerglide a 3.55:1 gearset.

Regardless, the Super Turbo-Fire '56 was the fastest Chevy yet and one of the year's quickest production cars at any price. *R&T*, for example, shaved 0.7-second off the 0–60 mph time of its overdrive-equipped '55 (which had the short final drive, of course) and 0.8-second off the quarter-mile clocking. Concluded the editors: "The 14-percent increase in horsepower more than offsets the 10-percent [difference in axle ratios]." *Motor Life* concurred: "The new powerpack [*sic*] was noticeably livelier than last year's 180-bhp job at turnpike speeds... Where the new car should make its

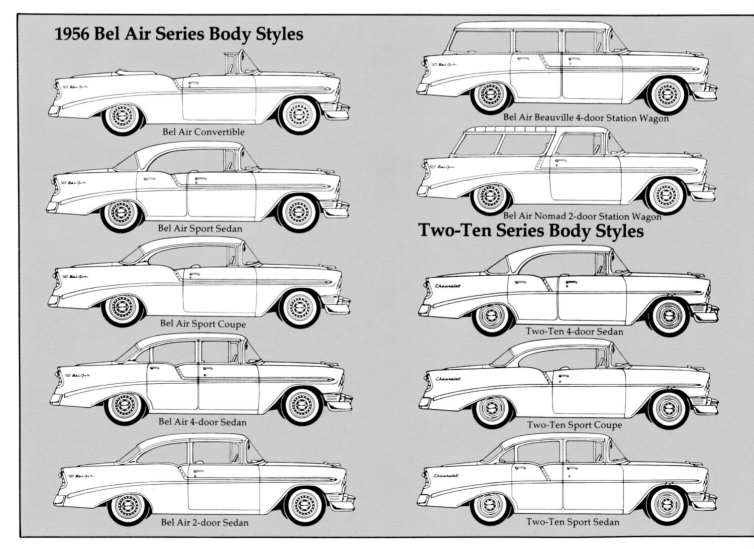

1956 Bel Air Series Body Styles

Bel Air Convertible

Bel Air Sport Sedan

Bel Air Sport Coupe

Bel Air 4-door Sedan

Bel Air 2-door Sedan

Bel Air Beauville 4-door Station Wagon

Bel Air Nomad 2-door Station Wagon

Two-Ten Series Body Styles

Two-Ten 4-door Sedan

Two-Ten Sport Coupe

Two-Ten Sport Sedan

biggest showing, 50–80 mph, time was lowered 3.5 seconds from stock '55 time, 0.9-second from the '55 powerpack's 12.9-second time."

And the 225-bhp version was faster still. Tom McCahill drove one, then wrote: "Chevrolet has come up with a poor man's Ferrari. . . . Here's an en-

gine that can wind up tighter than the E string on an East Laplander's mandolin. . .well beyond 6000 rpm without blowing up like a pigeon egg in a shotgun barrel."

McCahill judged Chevy the year's "best performance buy in the world," while *Motor Life* said it offered the

The Bel Air Sport Sedan (*above left*) cut a dashing figure in Onyx Black over Crocus Yellow, one of 13 two-tone color offerings available for that model in 1956. On the other hand, the Two-Ten four-door sedan (*above*) cast a more conservative image in India Ivory and Dawn Gray, although with 12 choices it too could be ordered in most of the bright colors.

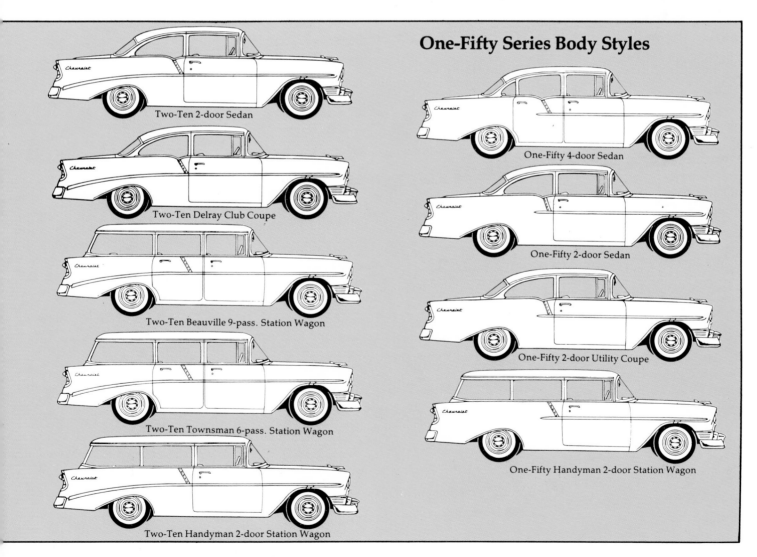

Two-Ten 2-door Sedan

Two-Ten Delray Club Coupe

Two-Ten Beauville 9-pass. Station Wagon

Two-Ten Townsman 6-pass. Station Wagon

Two-Ten Handyman 2-door Station Wagon

One-Fifty Series Body Styles

One-Fifty 4-door Sedan

One-Fifty 2-door Sedan

One-Fifty 2-door Utility Coupe

One-Fifty Handyman 2-door Station Wagon

1956 Accessories

All-Weather air conditioning
Fender antenna
Autronic Eye headlamp control
Seatbelts
Self deicing wiper blade
Wiring junction block
Power brakes
Locking gas cap
Continental wheel carrier
Electric clock
Compass
Nylon/plastic/fiber seat covers
Accelerator pedal cover
Wheel covers
Wire wheel covers
Tissue dispenser
Exhaust extension
License plate frame
Glareshades
Fender guards
Tinted safety glass
Door edge guards
Heater and defroster
Vibrator horn
Tool kit
Kool Kooshions
Back-up lamps

Courtesy lamps
Cigarette lighter
Floor mats
Outside rearview mirror
Non-glare rearview mirror
Visor vanity mirror
Body sill moulding
Front fender top moulding
Radio: manual, push-button, or
    signal-seeking
Automatic top raiser (convertible)
Armrests
Safetylight and mirror
Radiator insect screen
Power-positioned front seat
Electric shaver
Door handle shield
Front fender shield
Rear seat speaker
Spotlamp
Power steering
Whitewall tires
Ventshades
Outside visor
Inside visors
Traffic light viewer
Windshield washer (coordinated or
    foot-operated)
Electric-power window lifts
Electric windshield wipers

"best performance per dollar." Gushed normally reserved *R&T*: "Without a doubt, the greatest charm of this car is its smooth, quiet-running engine. Even though the compression ratio is extremely high, [we found it] impossible to make it 'ping' on full throttle at any speed. . . .The surge of power (actually torque) is there at all times, and knowing the ultra-short stroke, one gets the impression that this engine would be impossible to 'blow up' even under brutal treatment."

Competition results soon confirmed the road test findings. Smokey Yunick returned to Darlington with a quartet of '56s for a 24-hour enduro; one finished at an average 101.58 mph, beating the previous U.S. production-car record (set by Chrysler) by 11.69 mph. In July, three cars prepared by Vince Piggins, recently recruited from Hudson by Chevrolet Engineering, contested the annual Pike's Peak hillclimb. When the dust settled, Chevy was 1st, 2nd, 5th, 6th, and 10th. Better yet, winner Jerry Unser, Jr. had leaped to the summit in 16 minutes, 8 seconds, 1:16 faster than Duntov's impressive late-'55 showing. Truly, the "Hot One" *was* even hotter.

It was also safer, though few buyers likely knew it. With an uncharacteristic lack of publicity, GM had standardized so-called "crashproof" door locks in mid-1955. For '56, Chevrolet added dash padding, seatbelts, and even shoulder harnesses as optional extras, again with little fanfare. But while archrival Ford loudly trumpeted its new "Lifeguard" features this year, Chevy pedaled mainly performance and styling. And as the sales figures proved, buyers much preferred added dash to a padded dash.

In fact, Chevy's big '56 sales margin over Ford—some 200,000 units for the model year—underscores a curious, but historic exchange of images between the two old foes. Traditionally, Ford had been the low-price performer, Chevy "old reliable." Now Chevy was "The Hot One" while Ford was seen as more safe and sober,

Plain Jane, perhaps, but by 1956 even the One-Fifty models sported side chrome, as on this four-door sedan (*top*). Body two-toning became available, too, but selections were limited to six. The sedan delivery (*bottom*), which was offered all through the Fifties, sold in small numbers, and is rare today.

enhanced by a timid '56 facelift and that celebrated—but ultimately unsuccessful—Lifeguard campaign. The situation would change somewhat for '57, due to the relative differences between very altered contenders, but we're getting ahead of the story.

Options continued to play a big part in Chevy's success, and a few '56 newcomers suggested that "USA-1" was looking upmarket even harder. Besides the aforementioned front seatbelts ($10.95) and shoulder harness ($9.95), the list now included a Cadillac-style automatic headlamp dimmer ($44.25), remote-control door mirror ($6.95), and rear-mount radio antenna. Air conditioning was still a luxury for most mid-Fifties buyers, but Chevy helped make it less so by

reducing its "Four-Season" system a sizeable $135—though at $430, it was still pretty pricey. Radio choices expanded by one, ranging from $63.50 for the basic manual-tune set to $105 for the push-button signal-seeking unit. Power windows and front seat were up $10, to $155, but power steering still cost $92, power brakes $38. Among low-cost miscellany were trunk and underhood lamps at $1.95 each, a $1.60 visor vanity mirror, nonglare rearview mirror at $4.50, and foot-operated or automatic windshield washer ($6.75 and $9.95, respectively).

In all, 1956 was a good year for Chevrolet, even if it was necessarily less spectacular than '55. And it brought a fitting change of leadership, as chief engineer Ed Cole was re-

warded for his recent efforts by being named to succeed Tom Keating as division general manager.

One writer accurately summed up '56 as "a year of transition" for Chevrolet. "While the 1956 model did bring a number of firsts...it can't compare with the offerings of the previous year or the succeeding one....With Chevrolet collectors focusing their attention principally on the '55 and '57 models, the '56 is often overlooked. It shouldn't be. It was a vital link [in] the marque's evolution." And in the development of the "classic" Chevy, which would reach its peak as one of the first collector cars to emerge from this decade. For performance fans and those who appreciate definitive Fifties styling, the best was yet to come.

1956 Chevrolet Specifications, Prices, and Production

Model	Overall Length	Curb Weight	List Price	Production
1956 (115-inch wheelbase)				
ONE-FIFTY				
1502 Sedan, two-door	197.5	3,154	1,826	82,384
1503 Sedan, four-door	197.5	3,196	1,869	51,544
1512 Sedan, utility	197.5	3,117	1,734	9,879
1529 Handyman, two-door wagon	200.8	3,299	2,171	13,487
TWO-TEN				
2102 Sedan, two-door	197.5	3,167	1,912	205,545
2103 Sedan, four-door	197.5	3,202	1,955	283,125
2109 Townsman, four-door wagon	200.8	3,371	2,263	113,656
2113 Sport Sedan, four-door hardtop	197.5	3,252	2,117	20,021
2119 Beauville, four-door wagon (9P)	200.8	3,490	2,348	17,988
2124 Delray, coupe	197.5	3,172	1,971	56,382
2129 Handyman, two-door wagon	200.8	3,334	2,215	22,038
2154 Sport Coupe, hardtop	197.5	3,194	2,063	18,616
BEL AIR				
2402 Sedan, two-door	197.5	3,187	2,025	104,849
2403 Sedan, four-door	197.5	3,221	2,068	269,798
2413 Sport Sedan, four-door hardtop	197.5	3,270	2,230	103,602
2419 Beauville, four-door wagon (9P)	200.8	3,506	2,482	13,279
2429 Nomad, two-door wagon	200.8	3,352	2,608	7,886
2434 Convertible, coupe	197.5	3,330	2,344	41,268
2454 Sport Coupe, hardtop	197.5	3,222	2,176	128,382

Engine/Transmission Availability

	cid	bore/stroke (inches)	compression ratio	bhp @ rpm	carb	trans
1956						
Six	235	3.56 × 3.94	8.0:1	140 @ 4200	1V	3-sp., OD, PG[1]
V-8	265	3.75 × 3.00	8.0:1	162 @ 4200	2V	3-sp., OD
V-8	265	3.75 × 3.00	8.0:1	170 @ 4400	2V	PG[1]
V-8	265	3.75 × 3.00	8.0:1	205 @ 4600	4V	3-sp., OD, PG[1]
V-8	265	3.75 × 3.00	9.25:1	225 @ 5200	2-4V	3-sp., OD, PG[1]

[1]Powerglide

1957:
"Sweet, Smooth,
and Sassy!"

The Bel Air convertible found 47,562 buyers for '57. (Owners: Roger and Betty Jerie)

Compared to the all-new Ford and Plymouth, Chevrolet went to market for 1957 with a heavily facelifted three-year-old car. No matter, Chevy had it right. The restyling was extensive—and superbly executed. Not only that, the now-famous 283 small-block V-8 made its debut. With fuel injection, it achieved the engineering milestone of one horsepower per cubic inch.

A facelift and more horsepower don't necessarily make a great automobile—unless it's the '57 Chevrolet. Almost from the day production ceased, it's been coveted not only as the last of the "classic" Chevys but the best—the definitive example of *Automobilis Americanis* in the fabulous Fifties. In fact, except for its Corvette cousins and Ford's two-seat 1955–57 Thunderbird, it remains the most collectible car of the decade.

In a way, this enduring adoration is difficult to fathom. Much of it stems from the undeniable performance of the newly enlarged, 283-cubic-inch V-8, and the presumed historical significance of the top, 283-horsepower version with "Ramjet" fuel injection (also available on the '57 Corvette). It was this development, of course, that prompted Chevrolet to claim an industry first in that now-famous ad headlined "1 h.p. per cu. in."

But Chevy partisans and most historians have long overlooked some salient facts. First, Chrysler achieved this ideal the previous season and *without* such exotica—just optional high-compression heads that gave its 354-cid hemi V-8 a rated 355 bhp in the 300B. Second, Chevy wasn't alone with a '57 "fuelie." Pontiac introduced a similar setup with its flashy, mid-year Bonneville convertible, and the Bendix "Electrojector" system was available (if rarely seen) from Plymouth, Dodge, DeSoto, Chrysler, even Rambler. Moreover, Ramjet was as expensive as any of its ilk and just as troublesome, at least initially, so it was just as short-lived, at least in the bread-and-butter Chevys.

But credit where credit is due. The Bonneville and high-performance MoPars were expensive rarities, while the costliest '57 Chevy—a Bel Air Nomad with everything, *including* Ramjet—sold for thousands less. Then too, only Chevy offered a "fuelie" on *any* of its '57s, right down to the cheap One-Fifty utility sedan. Yet you really didn't need it. Even in carbureted form, the 283 packed more power than the hottest '56 setup. And as this year's all-new Ford and Plymouth were both larger and heavier, Chevy continued to enjoy a substantial performance edge not just in the low-price field but industry-wide.

Which brings up another part of the '57's appeal, namely what Chevrolet became for '58: bigger, heavier, thirstier, and slower, costlier, less agile, and more Buick-like in ride, appearance, and appointments. Yet the

'58s sold relatively *better* than the '57s despite a much more difficult market.

Why? Because 1957 was not the banner year Detroit expected, and competition was fiercer than ever. Though total car/truck volume was up somewhat from '56, car output actually declined by nearly 85,000 units to just over 6.2 million, due partly to the start of a national economic recession that would devastate the '58 market. Styling again proved the deciding sales factor, and General Motors lost ground (from 52.8 to 46.1 percent in market share) by inexplicably losing its traditional industry design leadership, mostly to Virgil Exner's striking new Chrysler Corporation fleet. Against those cars and George Walker's equally new Ford and Mercury, the rebodied '57 Cadillac, Buick, and Oldsmobile seemed dull and conservative, while Chevrolet and Pontiac had only third-season facelifts.

Almost predictably, then, Ford outpaced Chevy in model year production by some 170,000 cars, Plymouth wrested 3rd back from Buick, Mercury and Dodge pressed Pontiac, and DeSoto and Chrysler closed in on Cadillac. Chevy's one consolation was nipping Ford in calendar year output and total market share, albeit by razor-thin margins: 136 units and 0.01-percent (24.90 to 24.89), respectively. With all this, *Motor Life* magazine was devastatingly accurate in assessing Chevy '57: "Never before has it had so much to offer. And as a matter of fact, never has it needed it more."

More was certainly Chevy's watchword this year. The big news, of course, was the 283 V-8, created by stretching the 265 bore 0.11-inch to 3.88 inches (stroke remained at 3.00 inches). It arrived in no fewer than six versions—two fuelies and four with carburetors—swelling engine choices from five to eight.

The familiar two-barrel, 162-bhp 265 continued as the base V-8 with manual shift, but the mildest 283 (also called Turbo-Fire) was now its automatic counterpart, sporting single four-barrel carburetor, 8.5:1 compression,

Opposite page: The basic shape of Chevy's '57 grille had been determined as early as May 3, 1954 (*top left*), and by August 3, 1955, design work on the car was pretty much complete, except for trim items such as side chrome, grille mesh, and hood "windsplits" (*top right and bottom*). *This page:* As of April 20, 1956, even the detail work had been completed (*left, top and bottom*). Chevy also bored the V-8 (*below*) out to 283 cid; with fuel injection it developed 283 horses.

and 185 bhp at 4600 rpm. Then came a Super Turbo-Fire quintet with 9.5:1 compression on all but the 283-bhp fuelie. The single four-barrel version yielded 220 bhp at 4800 rpm. Twin quads boosted that to either 245 bhp at 5000 rpm or 270 at 6000 rpm, the former available with any transmission, the latter a high-lift-camshaft engine limited to close-ratio three-speed manual. Fuel injection outputs were 250 bhp at 5000 rpm or, on 10.5:1 compression, 283 bhp at 6200 rpm; again, the latter was a high-lift-cam unit available only with three-speed.

Regardless of power rating, all '57 Chevy V-8s featured a number of internal changes. Longer-reach spark plugs brought metal deflection shields to protect wiring and plug caps from manifold heat, while upper blocks employed thicker castings to prevent cylinder wall distortion from over-tightening of the hold-down bolts. Fuel passages were newly tapered, increasing in cross-section toward the intake ports and in the "ram's horn" exhaust manifold for improved scavenging and volumetric efficiency. And there were new carburetor fuel filters, larger ports, wider main bearings, stainless-steel expanders for piston oil-control rings, and a choke relocated to improve hot starting. Dual-exhaust engines now got a balance tube that equalized flow so that both mufflers would have approximately the same service life.

The six-cylinder "Blue Flame 140" returned with a more compact air cleaner and a flatter radiator top with side-mount water fill, both dictated by the lower '57 hoodline. More functional was a new fuel strainer on the carburetor inlet to supplement the gas tank filter, thus reducing the chances of stalling due to clogging from foreign matter.

Chassis changes began with updated electrics across-the-board: relocated battery and voltage regulator, line fuses for lamp circuits in cars without the accessory junction box, a chassis wiring harness with separate

units connected by multi-plugs, a new distributor for V-8s. High-torque clutches were specified for all power-teams save manual-shift 283s with injection or four-barrel carb, where a new semi-centrifugal unit was adopted. Mileage considerations prompted higher (numerically lower) final drive ratios for all but the optional stick/overdrive transmission (still 4.11:1). The manual three-speed now drove through a standard 3.55:1 gearset (the previous 3.70 cog was optional), while the automatic ratio was 3.34:1 (instead of 3.55).

As elsewhere in the industry this year, Chevy switched from 15- to 14-inch wheels and fitted low-pressure tires, reducing overall height 0.4- to 0.7-inch depending on model. Width and wheelbase were unchanged, but overall length was now 200 inches across the board, so the frame was strengthened with new front braces. Shocks were also revised to match the heavier bodies, power control-arm ball-joint and seal assemblies were adopted for the front suspension, and rear springs were again moved a bit further outboard for handling stability. Front brakes were treated to new heat-resistant linings and stiffer pull-back springs on secondary shoes.

"The biggest auto news of 1957" was Ramjet fuel injection, manufactured by GM's Rochester carburetor division and developed by John Dolza, E. A. Kehoe, Donald Stoltman, and Corvette chief engineer Zora Arkus-Duntov. A mechanical system, it was what we'd now call a continuous-flow multi-point type, with a separate injector for each cylinder, plus special fuel meter, manifold assembly, and air meter replacing the normal carburetor and intake manifold.

Chevy's 1957 dealer sales book described Ramjet's operation as follows: "The basic principle of fuel injection is to deliver fuel directly to [the] cylinder in just the right amount and under precisely controlled conditions . . . .

[The injectors, or nozzles] atomize the gasoline, aiming it directly at the intake ports in a pressurized spray. The amount of fuel delivered depends on the air flow, which in turn is controlled by the accelerator. Outside air . . . flows through a special chamber which divides into separate tubes, called ram tubes, one leading to each cylinder. As the air approaches the cylinder, it mixes with fuel being continuously sprayed from the nozzle, carrying the atomized fuel directly into the cylinder in a precisely controlled air/fuel ratio. [A] fuel pump delivers fuel to each nozzle by a pressurizing pump from the fuel reservoir through a regulating system that meters it to

the cylinders." A special two-piece aluminum manifold casting carried the air passages and air/fuel metering bases in its upper half, while the lower contained the ram tubes and covered the top center of the engine.

Ramjet was touted as having several advantages: "increased power, instant accelerator response, faster cold starts, smoother engine warmup, elimination of carburetor icing . . . and better overall fuel economy." Volumetric efficiency was undoubtedly superior, fuelies having about five more horsepower than a comparable twin-four-barrel engine with no other changes. As there was no carburetor, of course, Chevy also claimed that FI reduced

stalling tendencies from momentary fuel starvation. To handle their extra power, fuelies got mechanical instead of hydraulic lifters, thicker front and intermediate main bearings (by 0.063-inch), and a special distributor with breaker points directly above the shaft bearing to help reduce gap fluctuations.

Chevy's other big engineering news for '57 was a second automatic transmission. Called Turboglide, it arrived late in the model year as a $231 option for any 283 V-8 save the 270- and 283-bhp versions, and weighed 82 pounds less than the familiar Powerglide (now priced at $188). The work of engineers Oliver Kelly and Frank Winchell, it was a two-speed, five-element geared-converter type modeled after Buick's famous Dynaflow, with three turbines and twin planetary gearsets plus variable-pitch stator and a conventional torque-converter pump.

Turboglide sent power to the driveshaft via turbine rotation through the converter pump's oil supply. Differing vane angles determined which turbines rotated when. Decreasing turning force or torque from the first turbine brought the second into play, which drove its shaft and the output shaft through the rear planetary gearset and on to the third turbine. Ultimately, all three freewheeled as the car gathered speed. Flooring the accelerator activated a kickdown feature that increased stator pitch for increased torque to the output shaft. Turboglide also incorporated a "Hill Retarder" (indicated by "HR" on the shift quadrant) that helped slow the car on steep descents by inducing drag on the rear wheels via turbulence in the converter-pump oil.

Unfortunately, Turboglide proved a nightmare for both customers and mechanics, prone to failure and difficult to repair. Too bad, because according to *Mechanix Illustrated*'s Tom McCahill, it was "as smooth as velvet under-

Opposite page: Chevy's four-door hardtop scored a hit in 1956, and was even more popular for 1957, with 137,672 Bel Air Sport Sedans built. (Owner: Bill Bodnarchuk) *This page:* Fuel injection was introduced on Chevy's 1957 models. It was expensive, but the top version developed 283 horsepower—one horsepower per cubic inch. "Fuelie" Chevys were rare even in 1957, and command top prices today. (Owner: Bill Bodnarchuk)

pants" when working properly. Years later, Chevy engineer Vince Piggins opined that "there was very little need of another transmission, and it was expensive to build." After persisting with it through 1961, Chevy reverted to Powerglide alone through 1965, then added the more reliable Turbo-Hydra-Matic already used by sister GM divisions. Said Piggins: "It would have taken a few more years to really get Turboglide to the reliability stage that Hydra-Matic had already

achieved, and sales being what they were, it just didn't make sense."

Though Chevy's '57 engineering changes were extensive, they were expected in the Fifties, when sales considerations dictated expansive—and thus expensive—makeovers for the last year of an existing design. Styling was even more important to sales and thus got even more attention, so Chevy again received a substantial and costly facelift, even though a complete redesign was scheduled for '58.

Part of this reflected Chevy's awareness of the all-new '57 Ford and Plymouth, though they actually affected 1958–59 developments more than '57 styling. But as former studio head Clare MacKichan later observed: "We just had no choice [but] to carry the line out until 1958, [so we] were as extreme as we could be while saving the deck, roof, and doors. Those were the established ground rules. [Yet] there was a great deal of pressure on us [to add distinction] to the '57."

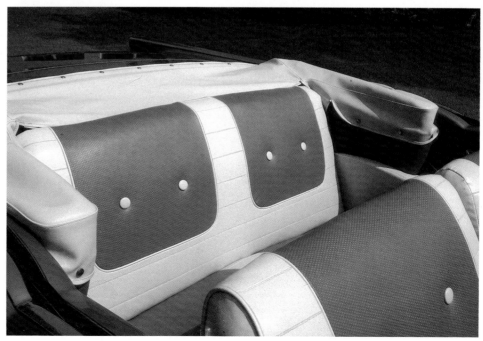

Above: The '57 convertible looked good even with the top up. Some thought the grille design a bit heavy, but it showed a certain Cadillac influence that didn't hurt sales one bit. (Owner: Bill Bodnarchuk) Although fins were the rage in 1957, Chevrolet handled them very modestly (*top right*), more through suggestion than reality. The dashboard (*right center*) was completely redone for '57, with dials placed up high for easy readability. Although interiors could be quite spartan on low-price One-Fifty models, Bel Airs (*bottom right*) sported attractive, colorful, and durable materials. (Owner: George Paul)

They succeeded by invoking ideas tried long before. The '57's massive new bumper/grille, for example, had been evident in various sketches since 1949, and one 1953 Carl Renner rendering was surprisingly close to the eventual production design. High cost—and styling chief Harley Earl's wishes—precluded it on the '55, but a sizeable budget made it possible for '57, "when they [finally] had money to do something quite radical for Chevrolet," as Renner recalled.

Not that the stylists worried about money. "I think today there's a little more awareness of that," MacKichan told *COLLECTIBLE AUTOMOBILE*® magazine in 1984. "But at that time, chief designers didn't have that under their wings. There would be much direction from Chevrolet Division... and Earl would pass down statements on whether we were getting into trouble. But other than that, we didn't concern ourselves. Our main thing was to get the design right."

Reflecting on his "classic Chevy" efforts, MacKichan told *COLLECTIBLE AUTOMOBILE*® that there wasn't much "continuity in thinking" from one year to the next. But as the '56 facelift had evolved from stillborn '55 ideas, "some of the ideas we worked on for the '56 [showed] up on the '57. I think by the time we got to [that] the feeling for exterior ornamentation was even stronger.... Amazingly, Harley Earl liked [the Bel Air's aluminum bodyside] panels very much, whereas with the '55 he wanted a very clean car."

Chevy's '57 facelift was carefully detailed for a longer, lower look, which, as mentioned, was no illusion. Cowl height was reduced with a new ventilation system featuring fresh-air intakes in the headlamp eyebrows feeding long, concealed ducts to the interior, one of the car's more radical features. This led to a lower hood, with twin "lance-shaped windsplits" instead of a central ornament. The new bumper/grille was dominated by a thick horizontal bar with a large Chevy

Opposite page: The 1957 Bel Air Sport coupe listed for $2299, but could easily top $3000 with a full complement of options, such as V-8, automatic, air conditioning, and power steering and brakes. Nonetheless, it represented excellent value back then and sold very well indeed. (Owners: Ron and Linda Jeurgens)

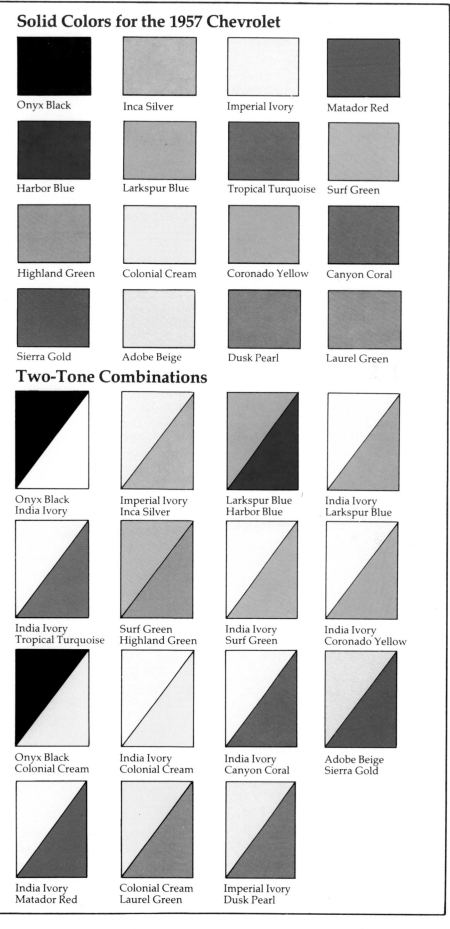

Solid Colors for the 1957 Chevrolet

Onyx Black — Inca Silver — Imperial Ivory — Matador Red

Harbor Blue — Larkspur Blue — Tropical Turquoise — Surf Green

Highland Green — Colonial Cream — Coronado Yellow — Canyon Coral

Sierra Gold — Adobe Beige — Dusk Pearl — Laurel Green

Two-Tone Combinations

Onyx Black / India Ivory — Imperial Ivory / Inca Silver — Larkspur Blue / Harbor Blue — India Ivory / Larkspur Blue

India Ivory / Tropical Turquoise — Surf Green / Highland Green — India Ivory / Surf Green — India Ivory / Coronado Yellow

Onyx Black / Colonial Cream — India Ivory / Colonial Cream — India Ivory / Canyon Coral — Adobe Beige / Sierra Gold

India Ivory / Matador Red — Colonial Cream / Laurel Green — Imperial Ivory / Dusk Pearl

crest in the center and small, circular parking lamps at each end, set against a mesh background. The bumper was scooped into a wide U, then flared up and out into bomb-like guards at the grille extremities. These were normally flat-faced, but could be fitted with optional black-rubber tips. It all added up to a fully fresh face, though stylists deemed it heavy next to 1955–56 appearance.

Elsewhere, the '57 not only looked different than the '56 but, to most eyes, better. Bodyside trim was adroitly handled. One-Fiftys continued with a short vertical "slash" molding at the beltline dip, meeting a half-length horizontal bar running back along the upper flanks. Two-Tens wore a sloping full-length strip that split just aft of the notch into a wedge, painted to match roof color on two-tone cars. Bel Airs had the same but filled the wedge with brushed alumi-

Interior Color and Trim Selections for the 1957 Chevrolet

BEL AIR MODELS

Convertible

Ivory Vinyl

Beige Vinyl

Turquoise Pattern Vinyl

Copper Pattern Vinyl

Yellow Vinyl

Red Vinyl

Silver Pattern Vinyl

Silver Pattern Vinyl

CONVERTIBLE TOP FABRICS

Ivory Vinyl-Colored Fabric

Black Vinyl-Colored Fabric

Light Blue Vinyl-Colored Fabric

Medium Green Vinyl-Colored Fabric

Beige Vinyl-Colored Fabric

BEL AIR MODELS

2-Door and 4-Door Sedans;
Sport Coupe and Sport Sedan; Townsman
Station Wagon; Nomad Station Wagon

Light Turquoise Vinyl

Beige Vinyl

Ivory Vinyl

Black and Turquoise Pattern Cloth

Black and Copper Pattern Cloth

Silver Pattern Vinyl

Yellow Vinyl

Red Vinyl

Light Green Vinyl

Light Blue Vinyl

Black and Yellow Pattern Cloth

Black and Red Pattern Cloth

Dark Green Pattern Vinyl

Dark Blue Pattern Vinyl

Opposite page: Compared to the more up-market Bel Air, the Two-Ten Sport Sedan sold poorly; only 16,178 were built for '57. *This page:* The same held true for the Two-Ten Sport Coupe (*above*)—production totaled 22,631. Station wagons had become highly popular by the mid Fifties, and Chevrolet marketed 214,632 of them for 1957 under the names Handyman, Townsman, Beauville, and Nomad. A Two-Ten Beauville is pictured (*right*).

num, one of Harley Earl's favorite materials. The decision to give Two-Tens the upper molding that defined the wedge apparently came very late, as some early press pictures show just the single full-length strip, two-toned below to match the roof.

Out back were reshaped fenders incorporating modest blade fins to accentuate the lower front end—and keep up with the competition. Tail lamps took the form of a half-moon at the base of each fin just above the bumper, which jutted out into oval pods for the optional backup lamps. Directly below were inverted half-moons painted black. These were intended for the backup lamps, as stylists had wanted to route the exhausts through the bumper pods. But a similar treatment had caused soot deposits on the '56 Corvette, so the backup lamps were moved up, their original housings filled in, and exhaust tips placed below the bumper. The '56's concealed fuel filler returned as a side-hinged panel in the left fin's vertical edge molding, just above the tail lamp.

Inside was a new asymmetrical "Command Post" dashboard (also called "Flight Panel"), with a raised cluster ahead of the wheel housing a large, circular speedometer between smaller-diameter water temperature and fuel gauges. Minor switchgear was arrayed below. Radios were still mounted centrally, above the glovebox, but the front speaker now faced upward from the middle of the dash top instead of directly at the right front passenger, and the panel was slightly concave all the way across instead of flat. Revised seat and door panel trim gave Two-Tens patterned cloth and vinyl (all vinyl on the Delray club

BEL AIR MODELS	TWO-TEN MODELS 2-Door Sedan, 4-Door Sedan, Sport Coupe, Sport Sedan	TWO-TEN MODELS Two-Ten Delray Club Coupe	ONE-FIFTY MODELS 2-Door Sedan, 4-Door Sedan, Utility Sedan
Silver Vinyl / Black and Silver Pattern Cloth	Ivory Vinyl / Charcoal Pattern Cloth	Ivory Vinyl / Charcoal Pattern Vinyl	Black Vinyl / Black and Gray Pattern Cloth

Handyman Station Wagon

Light Green Vinyl / Black and Green Pattern Cloth	Light Blue Vinyl / Black and Blue Pattern Cloth	Light Green Vinyl / Dark Green Pattern Cloth	Light Blue Vinyl / Dark Blue Pattern Cloth	Light Green Vinyl / Dark Green Pattern Vinyl	Beige Vinyl / Copper Pattern Vinyl	Black Vinyl / Black and Gray Pattern Vinyl	Dark Green Vinyl / Green and Gray Pattern Vinyl

coupe). Vinyl and loomed Jacquard cloth dressed Bel Airs, which had full carpeting as standard.

The '57 options sheet read much like the '56 edition except for Turboglide, the new engines, and generally lower prices. For example, power steering was now $70, down $22, and A/C was $5 less at $425, though power brakes were up $16 to $54. Power windows cost $59 for two-doors and $102 on four-door models, while a power seat was $43. Ford downplayed its Lifeguard safety features this season, but Chevy continued to list seatbelts and shoulder harnesses along with the usual extra-cost knickknacks, such as "Kool Kooshins," radiator insect screen, "traffic light viewer" (a small convex lens at the top of the windshield), electric or foot-pump windshield washer, spinners for the optional full wheel covers, and a new tri-tone horn.

Bowing on October 17, 1956, the '57 Chevy lineup (see chart) again listed 19 models in the three familiar series. The one model change was a six-passenger Bel Air Townsman wagon replacing the nine-passenger Beauville. Alas, the beautiful Nomad was in its farewell season as a distinctively styled "hardtop" wagon. Only 6103 would be built, the lowest for its three-year production run. Trim was again stock Bel Air except for Nomad script and a small gold "V" on V-8 tailgates.

Chevy ads aptly described the '57s as "Sweet, Smooth, and Sassy!" And despite this year's more muscular Ford and Plymouth, "the Hotter One," as *Motor Trend* called it, remained the hottest of the Low-Price Three. Even the base 283/Powerglide combo was capable of 11-second 0–60 mph acceleration. Walt Woron's 220-bhp/Turboglide car easily topped 100 mph, hit 60 mph from rest in 10.1 seconds, and scampered from 50 to 80 mph in 10 seconds. "Appreciably faster on all counts," wrote Woron, who praised Turboglide for its near imperceptible shift action and fine engine braking.

Later in the year, *MT* tested a Powerglide-equipped 270-bhp Bel Air Sport Sedan for a Chevy/Ford/Plymouth showdown. It clocked 9.9 seconds for the 0–60 mph sprint and 17.5 seconds at 77.5 mph in the standing quarter-mile. Scribbler Pete Molson termed these figures "impressive, particularly when you remember that we

had a low-performance transmission. It beat all the times of last year's powerpacked [sic] test car and all the times of the Ford and Plymouth this year except for the Plymouth's time from 0–45 mph."

All was not perfect, of course. Molson disliked the '57's "somewhat softer ride, with resultant greater lean on corners and less confidence for the driver. There is no question that the car looks and feels bigger.... We prefer the taut feel of the '56.... Front-end heaviness is evident in a mushier feel [though] Chevrolet has the best weight distribution among the three cars.... Normal highway dips cause it no embarrassment. When they get bad, it bounces (but doesn't bottom) and then recovers quickly with no oscillation...." *MT* also criticized early brake fade, but liked the new dash and continued to laud Chevy's easy steering and superior workmanship.

The fuelies promised to be the fastest regular Chevys, but few knew for sure because Ramjet was a very rare commodity. One reason was price. At $550, it was prohibitively expensive for a family-car option, especially one whose merits even the experts debated. (FI was a still strange novelty at the time.) Accordingly, it disappeared as a passenger-car option after 1958. Another problem, ironically enough, was its early announcement, which touched off a sudden demand for injectors from sister GM divisions and even other automakers that limited Chevy's own supply and thus fuelie installations. Sometimes, it doesn't pay to be first.

Thus, only a few hundred Ramjet engines were built for '57. Most ended up in Corvettes, where the option not only made more sense but was more palatable, given the two-seater's higher base price. According to *MT*'s Woron, the sports car did 0–60 mph in 7.2 seconds with the 250-bhp engine and stickshift, while the 283-bhp version easily exceeded 134 mph. With the latter engine, suitable gearing, and some 400 pounds more weight, a standard '57 two-door might have done 0–60 mph in about 8.0 seconds and 120 mph flat out.

At least partial confirmation was provided in 1976 by "classic Chevy" dealer Bob Wingate and his unrestored 283-bhp Bel Air Sport Coupe. With close-ratio column-shift three-speed, 3.70:1 rear axle, and less than 30,000

original miles, it was a scorcher. Though Wingate didn't time 0–60 mph acceleration, he did make four standing quarter-mile runs at Southern California's Irwindale Raceway. The results speak for themselves: 14.88 seconds at 103.86 mph, two identical runs at 14.75 seconds/103.6 mph, and 14.21 seconds at 104.01 mph—all in strictly

1957 COLORS	Bel-Air		
	2-door Sedan	4-door Sedan	Sport Sedan
SOLID COLORS			
Onyx Black	●	●	●
Inca Silver	●	●	●
Imperial Ivory	●	●	●
Matador Red	●	●	●
Harbor Blue	●	●	●
Larkspur Blue	●	●	●
Tropical Turquoise	●	●	●
Surf Green	●	●	●
Highland Green	●	●	●
Colonial Cream	●	●	●
Coronado Yellow			
Canyon Coral			
Sierra Gold	●	●	●
Adobe Beige	●	●	●
Dusk Pearl			
Laurel Green			
TWO-TONE			
Onyx Black / India Ivory	●	●	●
Imperial Ivory / Inca Silver	●	●	●
Larkspur Blue / Harbor Blue	●	●	●
India Ivory / Larkspur Blue	●	●	●
India Ivory / Tropical Turquoise	●	●	●
Surf Green / Highland Green	●	●	●
India Ivory / Surf Green	●	●	●
India Ivory / Coronado Yellow	●	●	●
Onyx Black / Colonial Cream	●	●	●
India Ivory / Colonial Cream	●	●	●
India Ivory / Canyon Coral	●	●	●
Adobe Beige / Sierra Gold	●	●	●
India Ivory / Matador Red	●	●	●
Colonial Cream / Laurel Green	●	●	●
Imperial Ivory / Dusk Pearl	●	●	●

stock trim! (He even ran with the air cleaner and street tires.) Fuel economy seems academic in this context, but Wingate reported 20.8 mpg—on high test, naturally—including travel to and from the track. "That figure, too, says an awful lot for fuel injection," he wrote, "because the twin four-barrel setups I've owned have always been pretty thirsty."

A major engineering development is never simple—or easy—and though Ramjet was a milestone in Chevy's brief performance history, bugs were inevitable. Vince Piggins noted that the injectors were "very prone to dirt, clogging, dirty fuel, and what not." Initially, they also absorbed enough heat to cause rough idling, later cured by extending them further into the air stream. Yet despite such teething troubles and slow public acceptance, Ramjet was soon developed to the point that it would continue as a Corvette option all the way through 1965.

And it served Chevy well during the 1957 racing season. In late 1956, an "in-

Exterior Color Selections for the 1957 Chevrolet

Sport Coupe	Convertible	Townsman 6-pass. Wagon	Nomad	Two-Ten								One-Fifty			
				2-door Sedan	4-door Sedan	Sport Sedan	Sport Coupe	Delray Club Coupe	Beauville 9-pass. Wagon	Townsman 4-door Wagon	Handyman 2-door Wagon	2-door Sedan	4-door Sedan	Utility Sedan	Handyman 2-door Wagon
•	A	•	•	•	•	•	•	•	•	•	•	•	•	•	•
•	A	•	•	•	•	•	•	•	•	•	•	•	•	•	•
•	A	•	•	•	•	•	•	•	•	•	•	•	•	•	•
•	A	•	•	•	•	•	•	•	•	•	•	•	•	•	•
•	B	•	•	•	•	•	•	•	•	•	•	•	•	•	•
•	B	•	•	•	•	•	•	•	•	•	•	•	•	•	•
•	A	•	•	•	•	•	•	•	•	•	•	•	•	•	•
•	C	•	•	•	•	•	•	•	•	•	•	•	•	•	•
•	C	•	•	•	•	•	•	•	•	•	•	•	•	•	•
•	A	•	•	•	•	•	•	•	•	•	•	•	•	•	•
	A														
	A														
•	D							•							
•	D	•	•	•		•	•	•	•	•	•	•			•
	A														
	A														
•		•	•	•	•	•	•	•	•	•	•	•	•	•	•
•	n	•	•	•	•	•	•	•	•	•	•	•	•	•	•
•	o	•	•	•	•	•	•	•	•	•	•	•	•	•	•
•		•	•	•	•	•	•	•	•	•	•	•	•	•	•
•	t	•	•	•	•	•	•	•	•	•	•	•	•	•	•
•	w	•	•	•	•	•	•	•	•	•	•	•	•	•	•
•	o	•	•	•	•	•	•	•	•	•	•	•	•	•	•
•	-	•	•	•	•	•	•	•	•	•	•	•	•	•	•
•	t	•	•	•	•	•	•	•	•	•	•	•	•	•	•
•	o	•	•	•	•	•	•	•	•	•	•	•	•	•	•
•	n	•	•	•	•	•	•	•	•	•	•	•	•	•	•
•	i	•	•					•	•	•	•				
•	n	•	•	•	•	•	•	•	•	•	•	•	•	•	•
•	g	•	•	•	•	•	•	•	•	•	•				
•		•	•	•	•	•	•	•	•	•	•				

Convertible Top Colors: A-Ivory or Black; B-Ivory or Light Blue; C-Ivory or Medium Green; D-Ivory or Beige

1957 Bel Air Series Body Styles

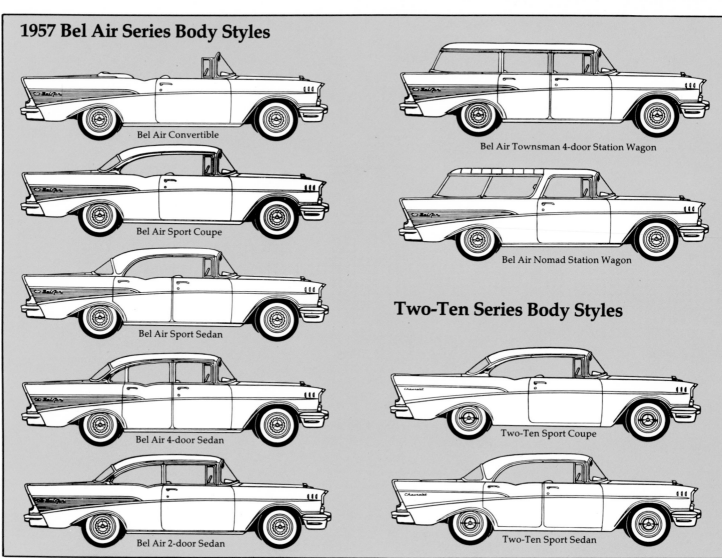

Bel Air Convertible

Bel Air Sport Coupe

Bel Air Sport Sedan

Bel Air 4-door Sedan

Bel Air 2-door Sedan

Bel Air Townsman 4-door Station Wagon

Bel Air Nomad Station Wagon

Two-Ten Series Body Styles

Two-Ten Sport Coupe

Two-Ten Sport Sedan

Except for the Corvette ($3465), and Nomad ($2757) and Bel Air Townsman ($2580) station wagons, the $2511 Bel Air convertible (*far left*) was the costliest Chevy offered for 1957. It came in 16 solid hues, and no two-tone paint jobs were offered; Matador Red is shown here. The top could be ordered in five colors: ivory, black, light blue, medium green, and beige. Seven different color combinations were available for the all-vinyl interior, such as red with silver pattern vinyl (*left*). (Owners: Roger and Betty Jerie)

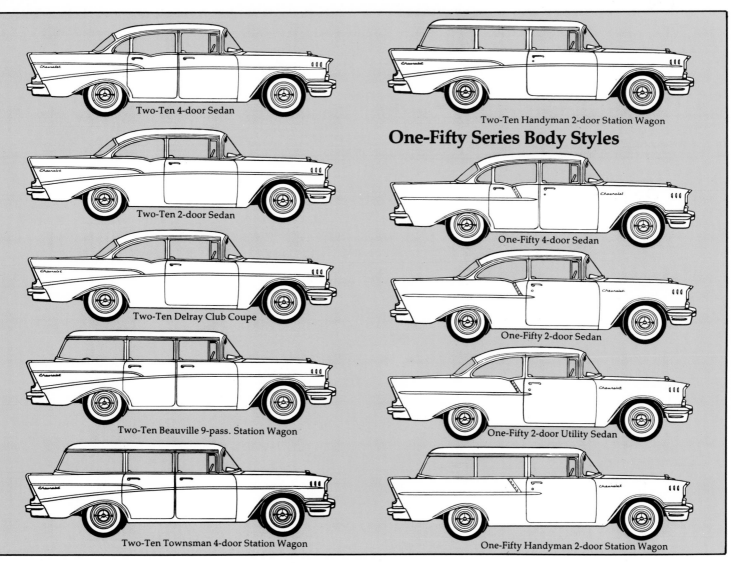

Two-Ten 4-door Sedan

Two-Ten 2-door Sedan

Two-Ten Delray Club Coupe

Two-Ten Beauville 9-pass. Station Wagon

Two-Ten Townsman 4-door Station Wagon

Two-Ten Handyman 2-door Station Wagon

One-Fifty Series Body Styles

One-Fifty 4-door Sedan

One-Fifty 2-door Sedan

One-Fifty 2-door Utility Sedan

One-Fifty Handyman 2-door Station Wagon

1957 Accessories

Air conditioning	Cigarette lighter
Electric fender antenna	Floor mats
Manual fender antenna, left and right	Outside rearview mirrors
Autronic Eye headlamp control	Inside non-glare rearview mirror
Front and rear basket units	Vanity visor mirror
Seatbelts	Body sill moulding
Wiring junction block	Lower trunk lid edge moulding
Safetylight bracket	Radio: manual, push-button, or Wonder Bar
Power brakes	Armrests
Locking gas cap	Safetylight with mirror
Continental wheel carrier	Radiator insect screen
Electric clock	Power-positioned front seat
Compass	Electric shaver
Full wheel covers	Door handle shields
Bumper cushion	Parking brake signal
Tissue dispenser	Rear seat speaker
Gasoline filter unit	Wheel spinners
License plate frame (chrome or gold)	Hand portable spotlight
Glareshades	Power steering
Tinted safety glass	Vacuum tank
Bumper guards	Whitewall tires
Door edge guards	Ventshades
Shoulder harness	Traffic light viewer
Heater and defroster	Outside visors
Horn with third note	Inside visors
Tool kit	Windshield washer (push-button or foot-operated)
Kool Kooshion	
Back-up lamps	Electric-power window lifts
Courtesy lamps	Electric windshield wipers

dependent engineering firm" called Southern Engineering Development Company (SEDCO) was formed with tacit division assistance and Vince Piggins in charge. It duly prepared a squadron of cars for the Daytona Speed Weeks in February, to be shepherded by Piggins and team manager Dick Rathmann.

They did well, to say the least. Chevy finished the two-way flying mile 1-2-3 in Class 4 (213–259 cid), the top car averaging 102.157 miles per

As in 1955 and 1956, the 1957 Bel Air Nomad (*above*) was both the priciest and rarest of all Chevrolets. It retailed for $2757, and only 6103 were built for the model year. The Nomad was probably a losing proposition for Chevy because so many body and trim parts were unique to it, particularly at the rear (*left*). Since only 22,375 units were built during its three-year run, it's likely that not enough were sold to pay for its tooling costs. Nonetheless, Nomad's unique styling and low production made it a collectible car early on. (Owner: Bill Bodnarchuk)

hour. A Ford was 4th—seven seconds slower over the distance. In class 5 (259–305 cid), Chevy took the first 33 places in a field of 37, with Paul Goldsmith fastest at 131.076 mph. Two days later, Chevy was again 1-2-3 in competition for automatic/four-barrel cars, the best being Al Simonsen's 118.460 mph. Chevy also dominated Class 5 standing-mile acceleration by finishing *1-18*, the last car 10 seconds ahead of the top-place Ford (19th). In all, Chevy scored a convincing 574 points to win the Pure Oil Manufacturer's Trophy, clobbering runner-up Ford (309) and third-place Mercury (174).

Then, a setback. While Chevy romped at Daytona, the Automobile Manufacturers Association (AMA) met in Detroit at the behest of the National Safety Council, the AAA (by now out of racing), and several of its own members, who insisted that the "horsepower race" and the competition emphasis in auto advertising were

breeding a generation of dangerous, accident-prone drivers. Accordingly, a resolution was prepared recommending that automakers henceforth not participate in racing, supply pace cars, or publicize race results. It passed unanimously in June. But this oft-called "ban" produced only a temporary lull. Ford and Chrysler were battling openly again by the early Sixties, and GM hadn't really stopped, providing under-the-table support while publicly declaring that it "wasn't in racing."

So Chevy never left the dragstrips or the stock-car tracks. In fact, on Labor Day '57, three months *after* the AMA edict, Speedy Thompson averaged 100 mph to win the Southern 500 at Darlington. Piggins' racing parts business flourished from continuing demand for heavy-duty "export" components, and Chevys kept on winning in '58. A highlight was another Southern 500 victory, this time by Fireball Roberts, who averaged 102.6 mph in his '57. (Chevy won again the following year, with Jim Reed in a '59 model.)

Which brings up an interesting postscript. Right after the AMA decision, Piggins issued a sought-after booklet, the "1957 Chevrolet Stock Car Competition Guide," with everything a would-be Chevy racer needed to know: HD equipment, body modifications, track chassis setups, competition tuning, spare parts, even how to register a race car, including addresses. This and more clandestine factory support contributed to a steady stream of competitive, often formidable Chevrolet stockers. By 1961, when the next generation of high-performance street Chevys was born,

"USA-1" was number one with hundreds of racers, amateur and professional. The staid, pre-1955 image was gone forever.

And with model year 1958, so were the "classic" Chevys. Ironically, the division had been looking upmarket since the first of this memorable breed, the '55, and its aspirations were now realized in the biggest, heaviest, most powerful Chevrolets ever. Symbolic of the new order was the Bel Air Impala, a lush convertible and Sport Coupe with Cadillac looks and luxury to match, and a four-door successor to the handsome Nomad, identical with other Bel Air wagons except for its tailgate "bananas."

Enthusiasts have long condemned

the '58s as the first of the larger and clumsier standard Chevrolets that would persist through the mid-Seventies. Today we can view them more kindly: right for their day, superior to most Detroit contemporaries—the start of a successful new chapter in Chevrolet history.

Of course, opening one chapter means closing another, and car lovers everywhere have long mourned the loss of the "classic" Chevys. But thank goodness for the memories: of powerful performance and elegant engineering, nostalgic styling and raw stamina, high popularity and historic impact.

Come to think of it, these great cars are still making memories. And that's why they always will.

1957 Chevrolet Specifications, Prices, and Production

Model	Overall Length	Curb Weight	List Price	Production
1957 (115-inch wheelbase)				
ONE-FIFTY				
1502 Sedan, two-door	200.0	3,211	1,996	70,774
1503 Sedan, four-door	200.0	3,236	2,048	52,266
1512 Sedan, utility	200.0	3,163	1,885	8,300
1529 Handyman, two-door wagon	200.0	3,406	2,307	14,740
TWO-TEN				
2102 Sedan, two-door	200.0	3,225	2,122	162,090
2103 Sedan, four-door	200.0	3,270	2,174	260,401
2109 Townsman, four-door wagon	200.0	3,461	2,456	127,803
2113 Sport Sedan, four-door hardtop	200.0	3,320	2,270	16,178
2119 Beauville, four-door wagon	200.0	3,561	2,563	21,083
2124 Delray, coupe	200.0	3,220	2,162	25,644
2129 Handyman, two-door wagon	200.0	3,406	2,402	17,528
2154 Sport Coupe, hardtop	200.0	3,260	2,204	22,631
BEL AIR				
2402 Sedan, two-door	200.0	3,232	2,238	62,751
2403 Sedan, four-door	200.0	3,276	2,290	254,331
2409 Townsman, four-door wagon	200.0	3,460	2,580	27,375
2413 Sport Sedan, hardtop	200.0	3,340	2,364	137,672
2429 Nomad, two-door wagon	200.0	3,465	2,757	6,103
2434 Convertible, coupe	200.0	3,409	2,511	47,562
2454 Sport Coupe, hardtop	200.0	3,278	2,299	166,426

Engine/Transmission Availability

	cid	bore/stroke (inches)	compression ratio	bhp @ rpm	carb	trans
1957						
Six	235	3.56 × 3.94	8.00:1	140 @ 4200	1V	3-sp., OD, PG[1]
V-8	265	3.75 × 3.00	8.00:1	162 @ 4400	2V	3-sp., OD
V-8	283	3.88 × 3.00	8.50:1	185 @ 4600	2V	PG[1], TG[2]
V-8	283	3.88 × 3.00	9.50:1	220 @ 4800	4V	3-sp., OD, PG[1], TG[2]
V-8	283	3.88 × 3.00	9.50:1	245 @ 5000	2-4V	3-sp.[3], PG[1], TG[2]
V-8	283	3.88 × 3.00	9.50:1	250 @ 5000	FI[4]	3-sp.[3], PG[1], TG[2]
V-8	283	3.88 × 3.00	9.50:1	270 @ 6000	2-4V	3-sp.[3]
V-8	283	3.88 × 3.00	10.50:1	283 @ 6200	FI[4]	3-sp.[3]

[1]Powerglide [2]Turboglide [3]Close-ratio three speed [4]Fuel Injection